CO

Introduction	7
Veterinary surgeon	9
Vets in general practice. Other openings.	
Veterinary nurse	15
Animal welfare societies	19
Working with dogs & cats	23
Kennel work. Dog or canine beauty work. Work with the Guide Dogs for the Blind Association. Work with Hearing Dogs for the Deaf. Dog-training and handling in the Armed Forces. Dog-handling in the police. Security services. Animal welfare societies. Dog wardens. Working with cats.	
Working with horses	30
Riding instructor. Groom/stable manager. Breeding. Stablehand/apprentice jockey. Working with horses in the Armed Forces and the police force. Riding therapist. Farrier. Other courses.	
Careers in ornithology	38
Scientific research posts. Warden/conservation posts. Education/information officer. Administrative posts. Other possibilities.	
Fish farming, waterkeeping & ornamental fish	45
Gamekeeper	51
Working with livestock in agriculture	54
Jobs in farming. Farm manager. Graduate careers. Small-scale enterprises. Agricultural testing and inspecting. The State Veterinary Service. Feedstuffs. Environmental health.	

Zoos & safari parks 63
  Zoo-keeper. Safari park keeper. Other jobs.
Zoology 67
Marine & freshwater biology 72
Nature conservation 76
  The Countryside Commission. English Nature. The Forestry Commission. The National Parks. The National Trust. Environment Agency. Other opportunities to do with nature conservation.
Animal technician 82
Other opportunities for working with animals 85
  Pet shops. Taxidermist. Working in the media.
For further information 88

just THE JOB

JUST THE JOB!

The *Just the Job!* series ranges over the entire spectrum of occupations and is intended to generate job ideas and stretch horizons of interest and possibility, allowing you to explore families of jobs for which you might have appropriate ability and aptitude. Each *Just the Job!* book looks in detail at a popular area or type of work, covering:

- ways into work;
- essential qualifications;
- educational and training options;
- working conditions;
- progression routes;
- potential career portfolios.

The information given in *Just the Job!* books is detailed and carefully researched. Obvious bias is excluded to give an even-handed picture of the opportunities available, and course details and entry requirements are positively checked in an annual update cycle by a team of careers information specialists. The text is written in approachable, plain English, with a minimum of technical terms.

In Britain today, there is no longer the expectation of a career for life, but support has increased for life-long learning and the acquisition of skills which will help young and old to make sideways career moves – perhaps several times during a working life – as well as moving into work carrying higher levels of responsibility and reward. *Just the Job!* invites you to select an appropriate direction for your *own* career progression.

Educational and vocational qualifications

A level – Advanced level of the General Certificate of Education
AS level – Advanced Supplementary level of the General Certificate of Education (equivalent to half an A level)
BTEC – Business and Technology Education Council: awards qualifications such as BTEC First, BTEC National Certificate/Diploma, etc
GCSE – General Certificate of Secondary Education
GNVQ/GSVQs – General National Vocational Qualification/General Scottish Vocational Qualification: awarded at Foundation, Intermediate and Advanced levels by BTEC, City & Guilds, Royal Society of Arts and the Scottish Qualifications Authority (SQA)
HND/C – BTEC Higher National Diploma/Certificate
International Baccalaureate – recognised by all UK universities as equivalent to a minimum of two A levels
NVQ/SVQs – National/Scottish Vocational Qualifications
SCE – Scottish Certificate of Education, at **Standard** Grade (equate directly with GCSEs: grades 1–3 in SCEs at Standard Grade are equivalent to GCSE grades A–C) and **Higher** Grade (equate with the academic level attained after one year of a two-year A level course: three to five Higher Grades are broadly equivalent to two to four A levels at grades A–E)

Vocational work-based credits	NVQ/SVQ level 1	NVQ/SVQ level 2	NVQ/SVQ level 3	NVQ/SVQ level 4
Vocational qualifications: *a mix of theory and practice*	Foundation GNVQ/GSVQ; BTEC First	Intermediate GNVQ/GSVQ	Advanced GNVQ/GSVQ; BTEC National Diploma/Certificate	BTEC Higher National Diploma/Certificate
Educational qualifications	GCSE/SCE Standard Grade pass grades	GCSE grades A–C; SCE Standard Grade levels 1–3	Two A levels; four Scottish Highers; Baccalaureate	University degree

INTRODUCTION

Working with animals appeals to a lot of people. This book tells you the basic facts about many jobs involving animals, and where to look if you would like more information. As in most areas of work, the higher the qualifications you gain, the more interesting and responsible the jobs that will be open to you.

Some things to think about

- If you love animals, it can be very satisfying to work with them.
- In many of the jobs, you're doing something really worthwhile.
- You can often get first-class training.
- The work is often dirty, smelly and physically demanding.
- Some jobs are very routine.
- Most jobs with animals are not very well paid.
- It's no good being too sentimental if you work in something like farming, veterinary work or animal research.
- Jobs can be scarce, and there's a lot of competition.
- Some jobs don't offer much chance of promotion.
- There can be health and safety risks.
- Some jobs require a lot of practical skills.

Try to talk to people working in the sort of jobs you're interested in – how did they get into it, what do they like and dislike about it? If you're still at school or college, try to arrange to spend your work experience trying out one of the jobs or job areas you are interested in.

Find out more about what qualifications you need for the jobs you want to do. For instance, what exam results will get you onto a veterinary science degree course? Offer to do voluntary work in a local wildlife reserve, animal rescue centre or kennels; that will give you an idea of whether you would enjoy the job.

VETERINARY SURGEON

> Veterinary surgeons care for animals by both preventing and curing diseases, and through the treatment of injuries. Most vets work in towns where they have a surgery and look after small animals like family pets; some have country practices where the patients are large farm animals. Other veterinary surgeons work in research or in teaching. All veterinary surgeons have degrees.

There are over 17,000 qualified vets on the register of the Royal College of Veterinary Surgeons, which is the body responsible for the profession.

The high academic standard required is not surprising when you think that a vet has to know about health and disease in a huge range of animals. One patient might be a domestic pet, the next a farm animal, and even zoo animals can come your way. Vets have to be surgeons and anaesthetists as well as 'GPs'. They do the job of a pharmacist very often, too, and need a detailed knowledge of veterinary medicines. If they work in private practice, as many vets do, then the ability to run a business is also required. It's a very tough job – physically demanding when large animals are involved, and tiring when there are night calls to calving heifers or injured pets. Of course, the financial rewards and job satisfaction can be very high.

Where vets work

- About half of all vets work in general practices with the familiar veterinary surgeries.

- About 300 work in industry for commercial firms.
- Over 600 work for the government State Veterinary Service.
- About 300 work for animal welfare organisations.
- About 500 work in universities and colleges.
- The rest work for the army, for zoos, for local authorities and a few other organisations.

What it takes

Veterinary surgeons have to be:

- dedicated to the care and welfare of animals;
- prepared to work unsocial hours – including nights and weekends;
- alert to signs of abuse or cruelty;
- good at watching for different signs in animals' behaviour;
- good at dealing with people;
- able to detach themselves from sentiment which sometimes surrounds cases;
- physically fit – especially when working with large animals;
- able to run a business and work out costs;
- content to work in all manner of surroundings – sometimes unpleasant;
- prepared to travel.

Sam – veterinary surgeon

'I got hooked on the James Herriot novels when I was younger, and was determined from then on to be a vet. The fact that I needed to work very hard to get high-grade science A levels, and the long years of study afterwards, did make me wonder at times if I had made the right choice. However, I now have my own practice, and I feel it's all been worth it.

You obviously must care about animals, but you also

need quite a strong stomach to do this job. I tested mine out before I started my training, by spending some days with my local vet. I did feel squeamish at first, but soon got over it.

One of the most difficult things about working with animals is trying to find out exactly what the problem is. I do wish they could tell me where it hurts! I have to rely on what the owners tell me, or on the animal's behaviour, which is not always reliable. It can take a long time to diagnose what is wrong.

I spend a lot of time just driving to and from farms, or people's homes, if the animals are too big or too ill to be brought to my surgery. This takes up precious time that I really don't have, although the veterinary nurse at the surgery does try to arrange several appointments in the same area to cut down on the miles. I tend to do my written work – research and reports – at home, after the surgery has closed.

I couldn't do my job without the help of a veterinary nurse. The one I have at the moment is very good. He does jobs like carrying out blood tests on the animals and sterilising equipment for when I have to carry out operations. He sometimes complains about having to clean out the animals' cages, but he actually seems to be as happy as I am in doing this type of work.

Vets in general practice

In a veterinary practice, two or three partners work together, assisting and advising with the general health, care and breeding of animals. The animals may be household pets, zoo animals or farm species, including horses. In towns and cities, work is almost exclusively with small domestic animals. In more rural areas, some practices are mainly concerned with farm livestock and horses, but others also deal with small domestic animals.

Other openings

About half of all vets do not work from a surgery. One advantage of posts outside general practice is that they usually entail more regular working hours. They also offer greater financial security, without the stress of running a business. However, vets who go on to more senior posts are likely to find that their job involves less and less actual contact with animals.

Vets in **industry** are likely to be employed on research into new drugs, animal feeds or pet foods. There are also posts with firms involved with agricultural livestock development. This type of work may involve experiments on animals.

The vets who work in **government service**, including the Ministry of Agriculture, Fisheries and Food's State Veterinary Service, undertake a wide range of duties, including the control of outbreaks of diseases which could reach epidemic proportions, such as foot and mouth disease.

Other vets are involved in supervising the **inspection** of meats, markets and processing plants. They are responsible for the welfare of exported animals during transportation, and other duties to do with the importing and exporting of animals and animal products. There are also some salaried posts with **animal welfare** organisations, such as the RSPCA and PDSA – see the section in this book.

Some vets choose to specialise in **research** – for example, in government laboratories, or university veterinary science departments, where they would also teach veterinary students.

Small numbers of vets work for the Army Veterinary Corps, zoos and other organisations, including short-term overseas posts.

QUALIFICATIONS AND TRAINING

The only way to train as a vet is to take a veterinary degree course at university, which takes five or six years. Entry is very competitive. More than 80% of applicants are turned down, so it is advisable to have considered an alternative course. Mature students are very unlikely to be accepted if over 30 years old. Graduates who already have a degree in another subject can be accepted, but may have considerable difficulty in financing themselves through a long course.

Subjects and grades

You need very good grades both at GCSE (or the equivalent) and at A level. The GCSEs are very important because, at present, they are the only exams which most applicants have actually taken when they complete their application forms. At A level, at least two grade As and one grade B are likely to be required. Chemistry must be offered at A level. The requirement for other subjects varies a little from university to university, but either one or two subjects from biology, physics and maths should be offered. Some universities feel that students without biology are at a disadvantage. You must check the prospectuses very carefully to find out what combination of A and A/S levels may be acceptable. Advanced GNVQ is not yet widely accepted for entry to veterinary science courses, but this might well change.

Course content

During training, subjects studied include: anatomy, embryology, physiology, biochemistry, husbandry, animal behaviour, pathology, immunology, pharmacology, virology, bacteriology, parasitology and toxicology. Medicine and surgery are studied in depth. The student must also learn about legal and public health requirements.

At all the veterinary schools, there is a period (usually three months) of experience in livestock husbandry. This is to enable students to gain an appreciation of farm management principles. All the schools' courses also include a training period of six months practical veterinary experience.

There are different emphases in the various courses. Some of the differences arise from the nature of agriculture in the areas in which the schools are located. You should look into course differences carefully, before completing your UCAS form.

Getting some experience

Veterinary schools will look much more favourably on applicants who have taken the trouble to find out about veterinary work and to get involved with animals on a practical basis. Try to persuade a vet to let you accompany him or her on a day's rounds, and to observe what goes on in the surgery. If you're really keen, the vet may let you help out at weekends and in the holidays. Farm work, helping in a kennels or cattery, or anything else which gives experience of coping with animals, will be invaluable to you.

just THE JOB

VETERINARY NURSE

> These are the people who work with vets in the same way that nurses work with doctors – in private veterinary practices, animal hospitals and treatment clinics. You can train as a qualified veterinary nurse if you have at least four GCSEs at grade C, including mathematics or science, or an equivalent qualification such as Intermediate GNVQ. Alternatively, you can start with the pre-veterinary nursing certificate, which does not require GCSEs. Animal nursing can be very satisfying, but on the whole it is rather low-paid work.

There are about 4000 veterinary nurses employed in the UK. As well as assisting in animal care, they look after the surgery and have reception and clerical duties. They sometimes give advice to pet owners.

Not all vets run a veterinary nurse training scheme: some just employ assistants who are trained on-the-job. You can't work your way up to becoming a vet, unless you go through veterinary training in the normal way, and for that you would need A levels as described in the previous section.

What veterinary nurses do
A veterinary nurse has to:

- receive the patients and their owners, deal with telephone enquiries and answer routine questions;
- file case records and keep accounts;

- clean and prepare the operating theatre, sterilise instruments, and make sure everything is in good working order;
- look after in-patients, feeding, cleaning and exercising the animals, and do things like changing dressings and removing stitches;
- assist at operations, handing instruments to the vet and helping with anaesthetics, under supervision;
- assist with putting animals to sleep if they are very ill or unwanted;
- produce X-ray photographs, do laboratory tests on urine, blood, faeces and other samples, and clip beaks, claws, etc.

Things to ask yourself
- Do you care about animals without being sentimental about them?
- Are you confident with animals?
- Are you prepared to help deal with all sorts of injuries, assist at operations and help with putting animals to sleep?
- Are you a good organiser?
- Are you good with people? Animal owners are sometimes in a distressed state.
- Would you like working some weekends and evenings to cover surgery times, and have time off during the week?

WHERE THE JOBS ARE

Most veterinary nurses work in small-animal practices (with domestic pets), but a few work with large (or farm) animals, in zoos, research departments and establishments, for pharmaceutical companies, or for animal charities.

Qualified or unqualified?
You can work as an unqualified assistant, in which case you would be trained by the vets in the practice you work for. Or

you can become qualified through the training scheme described below. Qualified veterinary nurses are able to apply for more demanding and better-paid posts, because they are trained in a wide range of skills.

THE VETERINARY NURSE TRAINING SCHEME

To enrol for the scheme you must:

- be over 17 years of age, and have your parents' consent if under 18;
- have at least four GCSEs at grade C, or an equivalent qualification. Subjects must include English language and science or mathematics;
- be employed in a veterinary practice which is an approved training centre, or have a written promise of such employment.

The training scheme lasts a minimum of two years and students work towards part I and part II examinations. There are some full-time, modular and part-time college courses which provide theoretical instruction, but, where there is no local college course, you can study from textbooks. Your employer would probably help you in your studies, as well as provide your practical training. Qualified VNs can go on to study for a Diploma in Advanced Veterinary Nursing (Surgical).

GETTING STARTED

A student post
The usual way to train as a veterinary nurse is to find a student post with a veterinary practice which is approved as a training centre by the Royal College of Veterinary Surgeons. If you can find work with a local vet not yet approved for training, you can ask if they will apply to the Royal College of Veterinary Surgeons for approval. Remember that practices do not often take on new students, so there is usually a lot of competition for posts. Experience with animals in any form – some weekend or holiday work with a veterinary practice, kennels or cattery for example – will greatly improve your chances of getting one of the few vacancies.

There may be other opportunities for school-leavers to train with an employer. Ask your local careers service for further information.

Full-time courses
A few agricultural colleges and schools of veterinary science run full-time courses, lasting one or two terms, which help to prepare students for the veterinary nursing exams. However, you first need to have spent some time as an enrolled student in an approved practice or centre.

ANIMAL WELFARE SOCIETIES

This section tells you about a few of the biggest societies and charities which exist for the welfare of animals, when treatment and care cannot be provided through private veterinary practice. These societies employ people to work for them, including veterinary surgeons, who are graduates of veterinary science. There are also opportunities for those with fewer or no academic qualifications.

Not many jobs with animal welfare societies are available, and they aren't found in all areas, as most charities have their main clinics and animal hospitals in particular towns, perhaps with smaller outposts elsewhere. Work with the welfare societies can be very satisfying, but it is not highly paid.

There may be voluntary activities which you can get involved in if you can't find a paid job in this type of work. Local animal shelters often need help with dog walking, general animal care, fund-raising and so on. There are also organisations involved with scientific research into welfare, such as the Universities Federation for Animal Welfare, and pressure groups trying to change attitudes to animal welfare.

The Royal Society for the Prevention of Cruelty to Animals (RSPCA)

The RSPCA is best known for its **inspectors** who investigate complaints about cruelty to animals. There are about 300 inspectors throughout England and Wales. The complaints they deal with include allegations against conditions in private houses, pet shops, boarding kennels, farms, markets and travelling facilities for animals. Inspectors are on call at night and at weekends. Some investigations lead to prosecutions, and others result in inspectors giving advice on how to improve conditions for animals. All inspectors have to be prepared to destroy unwanted and stray animals.

OPPORTUNITIES

To join the inspectorate, you should be between the ages of 22 and 40 (although occasional exceptions are made) with a good general education. A valid driving licence is necessary, and a medical examination must be passed. You also need to be able to swim 50 metres, fully clothed. Training takes seven months, combining theory and practical work. Inspectors who pass the training course can be posted to any part of the country. National Vocational Qualifications in Animal Care are available for employees and trainees with the inspectorate.

The RSPCA also provides treatment for sick animals whose owners cannot afford private veterinary fees, and runs homes for strays. Their hospitals and clinics in the London and Birmingham areas (like the one featured in the TV series *Animal Hospital*) recruit their staff through headquarters, employing veterinary surgeons, qualified and student veterinary nurses, hospital assistants and ambulance drivers. Hospital assistants need to be over 18 and must undergo six months' training on full pay. There are also a few jobs for kennel assistants, and managers of animal homes and clinics. Outside the London and Birmingham areas, each branch of the RSPCA is run independently and recruits its own staff. Much of the unskilled work is done by volunteers, so vacancies for paid staff are limited. There are also three wildlife hospitals, and the headquarters in Sussex employs 200 scientific, technical and other support staff.

The People's Dispensary for Sick Animals (PDSA)

The PDSA treats sick and injured pets whose owners are receiving certain state benefits, and cannot afford private sector veterinary fees. It runs over 100 veterinary centres, mostly equipped to perform major surgery. It also runs a Pet-Aid Service, where treatments are provided for the society by private veterinary practices.

OPPORTUNITIES

The PDSA is a major employer of qualified veterinary surgeons and nurses, and trains veterinary nurses. Receptionists are also employed at the centres. Mature applicants are preferred. There are some opportunities for work experience for young people with suitable qualifications who genuinely want a career as a vet or veterinary nurse.

The Blue Cross

The Blue Cross is a smaller organisation, employing fewer staff. It has fifteen sites in an area stretching from Yorkshire to Devon: three hospitals, two in London and one in Grimsby; a clinic at Wandsworth (London) and ten Adoption Centres – most of which cater primarily for dogs and cats, although two also include Equine Centres. In addition, the organisation has mobile clinics in Dublin which are manned largely by volunteers.

The three Blue Cross hospitals and Wandsworth clinic are approved training centres for the Royal College of Veterinary Surgeons' veterinary nurses training scheme. As well as appointments for qualified vets, veterinary nurses and student nurses, there are also some openings in the hospitals for ambulance drivers, laboratory technicians, clerical staff and kennel assistants. The Adoption and Equine Centres employ kennel staff and grooms, and the head office in Burford is the base for most of the organisation's administrative staff.

National Canine Defence League; Guide Dogs for the Blind and the Deaf

For information on employment opportunities with these bodies, see the section on working with dogs.

WORKING WITH DOGS & CATS

There are more opportunities to work with dogs than with cats; cat-lovers would say that's because their pets don't give as much trouble! Certainly there's more demand for kennels than catteries, as most people can find a neighbour to look after their cat while they're on holiday. And, as far as we're aware, cat-racing has yet to be introduced! You're not likely to need many qualifications for most of these jobs.

Man's best friend ...

The special relationship that exists between dogs and people means that there are opportunities to work with dogs in a variety of fields – with working dogs, racing dogs or domestic pets. There are many different areas of work where interest and aptitude are more important than initial entry qualifications. Some experience of dog-handling and training, with your own or other people's pets, is often expected.

Kennel work

Many kennels board dogs while owners are on holiday. There are also:

- breeding kennels;
- quarantine kennels;
- racing greyhound kennels;
- sanctuary and rescue kennels.

Kennel assistants feed, groom, exercise and clean out the dogs. Work starts early and weekends must be covered. In quarantine kennels, especially, you may learn about treating sick and healthy animals by helping the vets with inspections. You don't need academic qualifications, but you must be healthy, with lots of stamina, and experience of handling dogs is a big help. On the minus side, pay is often low but prospects can be good for those that stay in the industry. Young people in their early twenties often have responsible jobs with accommodation provided. Self-employment is also an eventual possibility, but this needs a lot of money.

GETTING STARTED

You could look for local work with training, or go as a working pupil to a good breeding or boarding kennels, or Bell Mead Training College for Kennelstaff. Ask the Kennel Club or the Animal Care Industry Lead Body for advice on courses and kennels providing training. Look out for adverts in the dog magazines and local press. Your local careers service will know of any training opportunities for young people in your area.

Dog or canine beauty work

Canine beauticians work from their own homes, or in pet shops, 'poodle parlours' and kennels specialising in showing dogs. They make dogs look their best by shampooing and trimming their coats, cleaning their teeth and clipping nails. They must be good at handling dogs and calming them if they're nervous.

Training may be given on-the-job if you work at a kennels or pet shop, possibly leading to a City & Guilds certificate in dog-grooming run in conjunction with the Pet Care Trust. There are a number of private courses advertised in the dog magazines, which is one way of gaining the necessary experience. It takes determination and practice to make a living as a dog beautician. While finding work with an existing firm can be difficult,

prospects for self-employment seem good, as not much capital is needed to set up in your own business.

Work with the Guide Dogs for the Blind Association

The Association has regional training centres at Forfar, Bolton, Exeter, Leamington, Wokingham, Middlesbrough and Redbridge, and a breeding centre at Tollgate. All staff need to be very fit, and also good at working with visually impaired people as well as with the dogs. Experience of paid or voluntary work with animals and/or with adults from various backgrounds will help your chances of employment. There are jobs in office administration and fund-raising as well as the jobs involving regular contact with the dogs. There is always a long waiting list.

Kennel staff are recruited from the age of 18, usually with GCSEs in English and maths or their equivalent, but motivation is as important as academic qualifications. There is an initial six-month period of training, followed by further on-the-job training of up to 18 months. There are opportunities to gain qualifications in kennel management or veterinary nursing, which offer a chance of promotion. Kennel staff are required to live on the premises. It is possible, in some circumstances, to transfer from kennel staff to guide dog training.

Guide dog trainers need to be over 18, with GCSEs in English and maths, supported by science, or equivalent qualifications. A full driving licence is required, plus evidence of relevant experience with both animals and people. New entrants share an initial two months' preliminary training with kennel staff, followed by another year or so learning training techniques. Once qualified, trainers are responsible for training dogs from the age of one year, until they themselves can confidently allow the dog to guide them whilst blindfolded. Dog trainers can be considered for further training as mobility instructors.

Guide dog mobility instructors are responsible for the final stages of training of the dogs, followed by a four-week residential course teaching the visually impaired person and the guide dog to work successfully together. This training takes place at the Association's centres, but it is followed up by visits to the client's home to monitor their progress. Applicants for instructor positions need to be over 21 years of age, with five GCSEs or their equivalent, otherwise the requirements are the same as for guide dog trainers. Training involves a three-year apprenticeship, the first six months of which are residential. There are two intakes per year of about six apprentices each, so competition for places is tough. There are opportunities for further training and promotion to senior and management posts.

Work with Hearing Dogs for the Deaf
This organisation trains dogs to react to sounds such as an alarm clock, a doorbell, a crying baby, etc, and to lead their deaf owner to the source of the sound. This is a much newer and smaller organisation than Guide Dogs for the Blind, but it is

expanding fast in response to increasing demand. The range of jobs is similar to those with guide dogs.

Applicants are selected on individual merit. All need to have experience of dog behaviour and training, and must have a caring and responsible attitude towards both animals and people. Applicants must have clear speech and communication skills. A knowledge of sign language is an advantage, but training will be given at the centre. There are no rigid exam requirements but a good standard of education is expected.

Trainee posts are residential and the minimum age is 21. A driving licence is necessary (and really a car, too, because the training centre is very remote).

Dog-training and handling in the Armed Forces

There are opportunities to train dogs and to work as dog-handlers or kennel staff within the Royal Air Force Police, the Military Police and the Royal Army Veterinary Corps. Dogs are used as guard dogs and for tracking and searching.

Dog-lovers should remember, however, that their main job in the Armed Forces is that of soldier or airman or woman. (See *In Uniform* in the *Just the Job!* series as a starting point for information.)

Dog-handling in the police

You cannot go directly into the police force as a dog-handler, but after the two-year probationary period, police constables have the opportunity to specialise to some extent. As in the Armed Forces, your job will be primarily one of law enforcement and only secondarily as dog-handler.

Police dogs and their handlers are both very highly trained – you may well have seen them giving displays of their skills. Handlers look after their own dogs, which live with them as part of the family. Handler and dog become an inseparable team – the dog is normally taught to answer only to its handler's orders.

Security services

Large security firms supply dogs with handlers to patrol customers' premises. Dog-handling is usually only a small part of a security officer's duties. The dogs are trained to protect whoever is handling them, but are not usually assigned to one particular security officer. With some big companies, you may be able to start as a kennel assistant and eventually become a trainer of patrol dogs.

Animal welfare societies

These have some staff specialising in work with dogs, e.g. kennel assistant with the RSPCA, PDSA, Blue Cross or members of the British Association of Dogs' Homes.

Graduates may find opportunities to research into dog welfare with the Universities Federation for Animal Welfare. A recent project of theirs has been to examine how the constant noise of barking in kennels affects the dogs' hearing.

The National Canine Defence League is a charity which specialises in caring for stray and abandoned dogs. Kennel staff are appointed by individual kennel managers. A list of kennels is available from the League's headquarters.

Dog wardens

Local authorities now have an obligation to deal with any dog problems within their area, including strays (any dog unaccompanied by a human). Duties include picking dogs up, transporting them to kennels or returning them to their owners and informing the owners of their responsibilities. It may be necessary for wardens to enforce the law relating to dogs, and to work closely with the police and welfare societies. You would also need to talk to schools and community groups about issues such as dog-fouling, so communication skills are important.

A dog warden must be able to deal with people and obviously be good with and understand dogs. A driving licence is essential. Jobs are usually advertised in the local press, or through your local authority. This is a job to go to after basic training, as most authorities and companies require people of at least 21 to control stray or badly supervised dogs in their area. They work with police and animal welfare societies as necessary. Wardens need to be able to deal with people as well as to be good with animals.

COURSES

Apart from training provision mentioned above, you will find various courses in animal care at some colleges of further education, including National Vocational Qualifications at NVQ levels 1 and 2. The Animal Care College offers correspondence courses in topics such as dog-breeding, training, judging and kennel management. The Pet Care Trust has a list of grooming training centres who are members of the British Dog Groomers Association.

Working with cats

There are very few opportunities for full-time work with cats. There are some openings in catteries which board cats whilst owners are on holiday, and setting up a cattery is always a possibility for self-employment. Quarantine kennels also offer work: some are for cats only, some for a mixed range of animals. Breeding cats rarely provides a means of making a living – most breeders do it as a sideline or a hobby. Animal welfare societies, veterinary practices and pet shops offer the chance to work with cats, amongst other animals.

WORKING WITH HORSES

> If you enjoy riding and looking after horses, you may be thinking of working with them as a career. Stable work is a way of life, not just a job. You have to put up with unsocial hours and all weathers. Instructors have to be able to get on with pupils – including the awkward ones – as well as with horses. But there is the satisfaction and enjoyment of working with horses and the open-air life, if you're really keen. Some of the jobs require a minimum of good GCSE grades or equivalent.

There are opportunities to work with horses in livery yards, trekking centres, breaking and schooling yards, hunting yards, saddlery and tack outlets, stud units and farriery work. However, there are some employers in the 'horse world' who exploit young workers and working pupils. Working with horses is rarely a well-paid job. You should check that conditions in a job are reasonable, including pay, time off, board and accommodation. You should also get a written contract of employment. A specimen example can be obtained from the British Horse Society (see Further Information section).

Riding instructor

Riding instructors do not *have* to be qualified, but most employers want staff to have passed exams, and pupils will expect instructors to be qualified to teach. There is a demand for instructors, but this doesn't mean that salaries are all that good. If you aim to run your own school, you need a lot of money to buy and equip the stables and horses.

TRAINING

The best way to become qualified is to study for the British Horse Society Preliminary Teacher's Certificate (BHSPT). There are minimum educational requirements for the Preliminary Teaching Test part of this, if you are under 18. These are four GCSEs at grade C, to include English language or literature, or an equivalent qualification. The exams cover equitation, stable management and minor ailments. The British Horse Society has further details.

You can train for the BHSPT Certificate as a working pupil or fee-paying student in a riding school or equitation centre. Details of BHS-approved schools are published in *Where to Train* (updated annually and available from the BHS). There are also courses available at further education colleges and colleges of agriculture (see the *Directory of Further Education*, published by CRAC).

If you don't have the qualifications necessary to take the BHSAI Preliminary Teaching Test, you can still take the BHS stages I, II and III and then complete the teaching test when you reach 18 years of age.

Holders of the BHSPT certificate must complete 500 hours of teaching experience before obtaining the BHS Assistant Instructor's (BHSAI) certificate.

The Association of British Riding Schools (ABRS) also offer teaching qualifications – at foundation and advanced levels (open to those with experience in good basic teaching).

More advanced training
Those who already have the BHSAI Certificate can study for more advanced examinations of the British Horse Society – Intermediate Instructor, Instructor and Fellowship. Details are available from the BHS.

NVQs, based on continuous assessment, are available in addition to the BHS qualifications already described.

Groom/stable manager

Stable workers are employed in riding schools, racing and hunt stables, show-event stables, studs and pony-trekking centres, and by the owners of showjumping horses. Grooms or stablehands muck out stables, feed and water horses and keep tack in good condition. Sometimes they get to exercise the horses. The work involves early starts and often weekend work and other awkward hours. You don't need exam passes to become a groom or stablehand, but obviously it is essential to like and get on with horses and also be capable of handling a great variety of horses and ponies in many situations.

QUALIFICATIONS

The British Horse Society offers qualifications for groom, intermediate stable manager and stable manager. They hope soon to introduce a qualification for competitive grooms, i.e. looking after, preparing and travelling with the horse for competition.

Candidates for the Association of British Riding Schools Groom's Diploma must be at least 18 and have had a minimum of two years' work/training with horses. They must already hold the ABRS Groom's Certificate and a first-aid certificate. The ABRS also offers Preliminary Horse Care and Riding Certificate levels 1 and 2. Both the Groom's Certificate and the Diploma are only open to people in work or training with horses.

Breeding

Breeding work varies according to the type of horse or pony being bred – everything from children's ponies to thoroughbred racehorses. It is possible to start without any formal qualification, though BHS and other certificates and diplomas can be very useful when applying for a job. A knowledge of biology and mathematics is helpful. The National Pony Society can provide a list of reputable studs. NVQs are offered, with most of the assessment carried out in the workplace.

TRAINING AND EXAMS

As well as some of the qualifications described earlier, the following courses and exams are relevant:

Diploma in Pony Mastership and Breeding (National Pony Society) – candidates must be 21 and have at least three years' experience at an approved stud. The examination covers breeding, presentation and riding, and agricultural management of stud land.

Stud Assistant's Certificate (National Pony Society) – candidates must be 17 and have had one year's experience in a reputable stud. The examination covers breeding, breaking, pony stable management, show production and presentation and, optionally, riding.

The National Pony Society also offers NVQ units accredited by the Racing and Thoroughbred Breeding Training Board.

The National Stud at Newmarket has two residential training schemes. The Induction Training for 16 to 18-year-olds leads to a NVQ level 2 in racehorse care and management. The Student Training Course for 18 to 25-year-olds leads to the National Stud Diploma. Some experience with horses is required, but no particular paper qualifications. Competition for the small number of places is tough.

The Thoroughbred Breeder's Association can also offer advice on training.

Stablehand/apprentice jockey

Although the term *stable lad* is used to describe the job of looking after horses in flat racing and jumping stables, it is of course equally open to females. Formal qualifications are not necessary, although many entrants do have good GCSEs or equivalent. The emphasis is on personal qualities such as fitness, alertness, confidence and the ability to work in a team. You will normally need to live away from home.

Most trainers prefer you to have had some experience of horses, but not necessarily riding ability. For most stable work, you should weigh less than nine and a half stone (60 kg) – although weights vary for flat or jumping work and especially for would-be jockeys. You start work as a stablehand, graduating from general mucking-out and labouring to being almost solely responsible for looking after two particular horses. This would include keeping them fed and their stable clean, as well as the more glamorous aspect of riding them during training as a race draws near, perhaps travelling to the races and even leading your horse into the winner's enclosure!

For those who ride exceptionally well, there is a chance to become an apprentice jockey (flat racing) or conditional jockey (jump racing). Very few go on to be top jockeys. Other job prospects include head lad, travelling head lad, veterinary assistant, trainer's secretary, etc.

To enter the industry as a 'lad', you can apply direct to a trainer, to the British Racing School or Northern Racing College, or to the Racing and Thoroughbred Breeding Training Board (RTBTB) Recruiting Officer. If accepted, you would commence a course at one of the two schools. Successful candidates aged between 16 and 18 can use their training credits to start training, which leads to NVQ level 1 in horse care, and level 2 in racehorse care. There may be opportunities to go on to level 3.

The regime of a racing stable is strict, and staff are expected to work long hours.

Modern Apprenticeships
The first Modern Apprenticeships in the horse industry, developed by the National Horse Education and Training Company Ltd and available from 1997, are specifically designed to offer young people a range of careers in the racing, breeding and non-racing sectors of the industry. Modern Apprenticeships run for approximately two years and are for 16 to 19-year-olds with a minimum of four GCSEs at grade C. They lead to at least NVQ level 3. Your Careers Service, local TEC or the NHETC can give you more information.

Working with horses in the Armed Forces and the police force

Horses are used by the Household Cavalry and the King's Troop of the Royal Horse Artillery. However, anyone joining one of these units is firstly a soldier, and only secondly a rider. These are combat troops, so at present are not open to women. There is no guarantee of working with horses throughout one's military service.

There are also opportunities to work with horses in the Military Police and in the Royal Army Veterinary Corps, and these are open to both sexes.

In the civilian police forces, mounted officers are used in crowd control and observational situations such as football matches, demonstrations, race meetings, etc. Not all forces have mounted officers, and opportunities are fairly limited. Nevertheless, highly skilled riders and highly trained horses are needed, but you don't have to be an experienced rider to apply. Remember that interest in, and aptitude for, the normal work of the police is of greater importance than the wish to work with horses alone. You will need the usual police entry qualifications (see *In Uniform* in the *Just the Job!* series).

Riding therapist

Horses can be used to help people with disabilities. Riding therapists may be employed by special schools, long-stay hospitals, and Riding for the Disabled Association centres. The Fortune Centre of Riding Therapy, in Dorset, runs a two-year Riding Therapy Diploma course (minimum age 20). Applicants usually hold the BHSAI, but this is not essential.

Farrier

Farriers often combine their work, which is basically shoeing horses, with blacksmithing (repairing agricultural tools and implements, making wrought-iron work, etc). You need to be fit and strong for farriery, and good at handling horses. Becoming an expert shoesmith involves studying the anatomy of horses' hooves and bone structure, as well as practical shoe-making. An interest in biology is, therefore, useful. Technical subjects also help, as apprentices often learn the general smithing techniques of gas and arc welding, basic engineering science, reading drawings and bench-fitting.

TRAINING

To work as a farrier, it is necessary to become registered, by serving a four-year, two-month apprenticeship with an approved training farrier and passing the Worshipful Company of Farriers' diploma examination. Apprentices require at least four GCSEs, including English language, at grade C or above. Candidates not in possession of the minimum requirements can apply to take an entrance examination. Candidates for the apprenticeship cannot apply directly to the Farriery Training Service, but must be proposed by an approved training farrier. Contact the Farriery Training Service for details.

It is also possible to train in the Royal Army Veterinary Corps, though everyone starts as a veterinary assistant before possibly specialising in farriery. Applicants (male or female) must be between the ages of 17 and 25.

Other courses

There are a number of courses in horse studies, horse management, equine studies, etc, at universities and further education and agricultural colleges. These are pitched at various levels up to a BTEC Higher National Diploma or degree. Look at the further and higher education handbooks in your school, college or careers service library for details of courses. Some courses are combined with business or secretarial studies. Most courses, other than degrees or HNDs, are only subject to discretionary local authority grants.

CAREERS IN ORNITHOLOGY

> There are not many opportunities for a career in ornithology. Jobs are generally not highly paid, but, even so, there is strong competition from very well-qualified people for those which do occur! The opportunities fall into four main areas: scientific research, warden and conservation jobs, education/information and administration.

If you seriously want to work with birds, you should do as much as you can as an amateur/hobbyist. Join the Young Ornithologists' Club, the Royal Society for the Protection of Birds, or the British Trust for Ornithology. Get involved with a local group and do as much birdwatching, studying, amateur survey and observation work as you can. You should get a great deal of pleasure from this if your interest is genuine, and it will certainly help when it comes to applying for those rare job vacancies.

Scientific research posts

There are a few permanent research posts for ornithologists, offered by organisations such as the Royal Society for the Protection of Birds, the Wildfowl and Wetlands Trust, the British Trust for Ornithology, English Nature, the Royal Society for Nature Conservation, and also bodies such as the Ministry of Agriculture, the British Antarctic Survey and the Forestry Commission. These organisations also offer temporary research posts, which normally last anything from three months to three years; projects often have links with neighbouring universities. In fact, most recruitment is on fixed-term temporary contracts, to help on a particular project. Success on one or more of these projects can lead to a permanent post.

It is sometimes possible to use research done as a case student with one of these organisations to gain a PhD.

What the work involves

Ornithological research means carrying out work such as surveying and monitoring the distribution and frequency of birds, often at particular sites and types of habitat, or areas under threat of development. Besides researching the bird-life, broader ecological studies and surveys of plants and other wildlife may also be required. There may also be opportunities to carry out species studies, for instance of species which are declining in number, or of birds such as pigeons and starlings which can cause economic problems because of their large numbers.

In addition to field study posts, there are also occasional jobs for scientists such as statisticians, who compile and analyse data which other scientists have collected.

QUALIFICATIONS

Research posts are mainly for people who have a degree (or a higher degree) in biology or another natural science. To take a degree, you will need a good background of school science – GCSEs at grade A-C in double science and mathematics, plus A levels (or the equivalent) in biology and preferably mathematics/statistics. A third A level, such as chemistry, geography or environmental studies, would be useful. Advanced GNVQ is accepted as an alternative for entry on some courses: check in the higher education handbooks.

Besides good academic qualifications, you also need to show a lot of enthusiasm and general knowledge of natural history, and it will be a great help if you have done some relevant voluntary work or amateur research. The RSPB publishes a leaflet which will give you some ideas in this direction (see the Further Information section).

Besides the graduate level posts, there may also be some opportunities for **project assistants**, who may be accepted with lower qualifications, especially if you can show enthusiasm and a strong amateur interest in, and knowledge of, birds and natural history.

Warden/conservation posts

There is a variety of work here, depending on the type and activities of the organisation offering the post. Centres which aim to attract the public to look at birds – like bird gardens for exotic species, the bird departments of zoos, and the Wildfowl and Wetlands Trust centres – offer posts which involve work rather like that of a zoo-keeper. The staff care for the birds and all aspects of their environment: it's a physical, outdoor job in the main, and involves not only looking after the birds and checking that all is well, but also work such as repairs to fences. Some larger centres employ staff specifically as carpenters or groundsmen/women.

Then there are posts for wardens at the reserves of the RSPB. Many of these reserves have a permanent warden, and sometimes a permanent assistant warden too. But the permanent staff are backed up by temporary staff to assist with summer (human!) visitors and all kinds of physical jobs, such as thinning scrub, repairing hides and maintaining records. RSPB wardens need a good standard of education, normally to A level or equivalent. A relevant degree would be an advantage.

There are opportunities for **voluntary wardens** (minimum age 16, to work for at least a week at a time) and **summer**

wardens (minimum age about 20 – paid positions, for which applicants must be available for the whole period between April and August). Success as a summer warden is a main route to becoming a permanent warden, or assistant warden.

More general warden posts (e.g. with the national parks) also offer opportunities for involvement with bird-life, though you need to have a really broad interest in natural history and conservation.

Rachel – bird reserve warden

'I am the warden of a wetland reserve which is managed particularly for the bird population that it supports. It is an area of shallow lakes and reedy marshland, which is the kind of habitat that has been much threatened in recent years.

My responsibilities include managing the habitat, surveying and recording the wildlife and organising visits to the reserve, both by individuals and by parties.

Managing the habitat is done to a plan drawn up by the management committee and is based on scientific observation and knowledge. Marshland is not a static environment and, left to itself, the lakes and marshes would gradually silt up and turn to dense scrubby woodland. I have to spend a lot of time organising clearing, draining and maintenance work. Some work will be done by contractors, other jobs are done by volunteer groups and quite a lot is done by me. Fortunately, much can be done in the winter when there is less pressure from visitors.

Because we are a bird reserve, we need to know what species are present and how the populations compare from year to year. This involves me in methodical obser-

vation and recording so that every year the management committee can make decisions about the running of the reserve. Being in the computer era, all this information goes into a database, so there is some indoors work, as computers and mud do not mix too well.

The other important and very different part of my job is the people part. Being in a holiday area, we get rather more visitors than some of the more remote reserves. We have hides for the visitors, with carefully arranged approach paths to minimise disturbance to the birds. I have also to take organised parties round the reserve. I need to be able to talk knowledgeably to all sorts of people, from primary school children to experienced birdwatchers.

I am very lucky to have this job, as they are difficult to get. There aren't many of us and there are always lots of applicants. I started off with a BTEC diploma from an agricultural college in estate management and I did a lot of voluntary work in reserves to qualify myself to get this job. Anyone wanting to do this sort of work needs to get the best possible qualifications and as much practical experience as they can to stand a chance. And as you can see from my story, you need to be an all-rounder!

QUALIFICATIONS

Qualifications are not essential for these jobs, though well-qualified people such as graduates do tend to apply, in the hope that experience as a warden may eventually help them in getting a higher-level post. Biological sciences and land management are useful subjects. However, practical and sometimes local knowledge can compensate for, or even be preferable to, high qualifications. In any case, practical skills and the willingness to turn your hand to anything are very important to warden-type jobs. Hours of work are likely to be irregular and long.

Education/information officer

Possible employers for this type of career include the RSPB and the Wildfowl and Wetlands Trust. There are also more general posts concerned with promoting nature conservation, rather than just those aspects concerned with bird-life.

Education posts are usually about communicating the work of the employing organisation to the public, often with a special emphasis on informing children of primary and secondary school age. The work of an education or information officer may involve: creating exhibitions, organising activities for school children, giving talks to visitors, writing literature and occasionally giving interviews for radio or television.

These posts usually require teaching experience plus a qualification in biology or another relevant science. Ability in graphics or other aspects of communication is often desirable, and personality is very important. There are also occasional posts in the editing of journals, which require similar skills (though some journalistic experience would obviously be an advantage for these).

Administrative posts

As with all organisations, those concerned with bird-life have work for administrators to do. There are the usual posts for clerical and secretarial staff, accountants, estate managers, souvenir shop managers, fund-raisers, and so on. It is really a matter of having the usual qualifications and experience for these kinds of jobs, and then seeking out an 'ornithological context' in which to use them. Obviously, an amateur interest in birds is likely to appeal to anyone recruiting staff for an organisation concerned with ornithology.

Other possibilities

As described above, under 'administrative posts', there are various ways in which you might make use of a keen amateur interest in birds by using the other particular skills you may have.

For instance, people living in areas popular with birdwatchers may get involved in the tourist or holiday trade, offering specialist activity or birdwatching holidays. You might be able to make a living from selling freelance articles or photographs to periodicals which specialise in birds. Or there may be openings with publishers who have a good series of bird books and who would welcome staff with an expertise in the subject. If your interest is in exotic birds, rather than wild ones, there may be openings in pet-shops or in breeding birds for sale. All these types of opportunities tend to rely upon seeking out chances and grasping them when they appear.

Of course, most people keep their interest in ornithology strictly as a hobby, and get great pleasure from it. It is certainly a hobby which allows you to make a real contribution to knowledge of birds and research into bird life. The British Trust for Ornithology, the Wildfowl and Wetlands Trust and the RSPB all have regular national and regional research programmes which depend heavily on the contributions of amateurs. There are also voluntary opportunities such as running a local Young Ornithologists' Club or WATCH group for children and young people.

FISH FARMING, WATERKEEPING & ORNAMENTAL FISH

> Fish farming – breeding and rearing fish in captivity – is a small but growing industry in this country, compared with fishing at sea. Some fish are raised in ponds, while others are reared in sea cages in open water. Managers and scientists have degrees or the equivalent. There are also opportunities for those with fewer or no academic qualifications.

Fish farming – the facts
- Britain has well over 500 fish farms.
- Most breed trout or salmon, but halibut, lobster and other fish are also bred for the table.
- Some fish farmers specialise in ornamental fish, or the restocking of lakes, rivers, reservoirs, etc, for sport.
- About half of all fish farms are in Scotland.
- The rest are found all over England and Wales, with concentrations in the south-west, Lincolnshire and Yorkshire.
- Many fish farms employ only one or two people and are in remote places.
- Most fish farms are privately owned and managed; other employers include the Environment Agency, which employs fisheries officers.

Like any job where you are caring for livestock, there is weekend and evening work. There are also seasonal busy peaks – at spawning and harvesting times.

Paul – fish farmer

'I built up this farm from the remains of an abandoned watercress bed. It has now been in operation for ten years or so, and specialises in rainbow trout. The only 'labour' besides myself consists of one or two students, gaining work experience as part of their training.

The work gives me a terrific sense of satisfaction – of course, this is partly because I'm running my own business. But besides the independence, I enjoy actually looking after the fish.

The job is very much a way of life. It's physically hard work and the hours are very long. There are seasonal jobs to be done, besides all the routine daily care of the fish. In spring, it's a 24-hour job rearing the young fish. Summer means cutting the weeds, which grow rapidly and would block the water courses. In autumn, when the leaves fall, they have to be cleared constantly. Winter means repair and maintenance work – repairing nets, tanks and machinery, and reconstructing the banks of the streams and ponds.

So there's a great deal of exposure to the elements. That's fine on a nice summer day; not so good at night, in a gale, when leaves and debris have to be cleared to ensure the water flows properly in and out of the ponds and tanks – blockages could cause the death of the fish. I haven't had a holiday since setting up, though in theory I could employ a relief manager. I'm basically self-taught, but these days I would strongly recommend anyone wanting to manage a fish farm to take a full-time course, such as an HND, to get a proper technical training.'

What the work involves

Hatchery workers look after the fish from spawning time to harvesting, and also look after the tank or river in which the fish are kept. Workers are often recruited locally, and there are no standard entry requirements. An interest in chemistry and biology and the possession of a driving licence would be an advantage. An amateur interest in fish would obviously be helpful.

Managers or farmers have general responsibility for the running of the farm, and would be concerned with bookkeeping and organising sales and transportation of the fish. A manager might be chosen because of experience with fish or because of high level scientific qualifications.

Scientific workers on experimental fish farms could be either trained graduate scientists, or technicians with a National or Higher National Diploma.

TRAINING COURSES

These are available at a few agricultural colleges: Sparsholt College near Winchester, Hampshire, offers the widest range. Courses include BTEC First, National and Higher National qualifications in fishery studies; BTEC and NEB qualifications in aquatics, aquaculture and gamekeeping and waterkeeping; and a BSc in Aquaculture and Fishery Management.

Entry requirements for these range from none for a First Diploma to at least one A level for a Higher National Diploma or two A levels/Advanced GNVQ for the degree. Scientific subjects are specified for National, Higher National and degree courses. Practical experience is a requirement for some of the courses. See the further and higher education handbooks for full details.

There are BTEC National and Higher National qualifications and courses leading to NVQs in subjects like waterkeeping, fishery management and fish husbandry or production at several colleges – usually agricultural colleges – around the country.

Holders of a National Diploma could be employed as technicians in the industry; an HND or degree can lead to a career as a technologist or in management.

The Institute of Fisheries Management runs a certificate and diploma course for members, covering freshwater biology, fishing methods, fishery maintenance and improvement, fish propagation, pollution, legal bailiffing and keeping duties.

Degree courses in aquaculture are offered at the Scottish Agricultural College in Aberdeen, and at Stirling University.

Degree courses in biological sciences are available with options in aquatic biology or fish biology. These require at least two appropriate A levels or the equivalent – such as a relevant Advanced GNVQ or BTEC National qualification – for entry. It is also possible to take a biology degree and follow this with a higher degree specialising in some aspect of fish biology.

Waterkeeper
Private keeping
In days gone by, the keeper's job was to provide sport for a few privileged people. Nowadays, many more people want to fish and keepers will be concerned with stocking their lake or river, rather than nurturing the wild fish.

Subjects a keeper would be expected to know about include freshwater biology, fish nutrition, selection and breeding, hatcheries and the legal aspects of the job. The job is not just dealing with fish: keepers also work with people. The fishermen are customers and must be kept happy, but, at the same time, tactful but firm control must be exercised about the number and size of fish that can be taken.

The keeper's job is vital to the success of a fishery. Unfortunately the pay does not match the responsibility. Wages are usually the same as for a craftworker in agriculture and, although most jobs nominally involve a 44-hour week, in practice much longer hours – up to 60 or 70 – may be worked. The keeper will often be earning less than most of the anglers who fish the water!

Water bailiff
Once in these much-prized jobs, people tend to stay put, and therefore the number of posts available each year is very small.

Water bailiffs are employed by the Environment Agency to enforce the laws concerning fishing (of which there are quite a lot), survey the river and be concerned with stocking, checking fish for disease and possibly netting and transferring fish from one place to another. They must establish good relations with local waterkeepers, police, farmers and landowners. Like waterkeepers, they must be tactful but firm in their enforcement of the laws and may have to deal with poachers.

Pay and hours are laid down as part of the Environment Agency wages and conditions, and overtime is paid. In general, the job is more secure and better paid than waterkeeping for private fisheries. The Environment Agency also employs conservation officers and technicians.

Ornamental fish

There is a thriving interest in ornamental cold water and tropical fish. Businesses dealing in this area are expanding rapidly, with over 2000 in existence.

Ornamental fish are sold to hobbyist fish-keepers, and they are also supplied to ponds and aquaria which form part of parks and other recreational facilities. The main job opportunities are to do with selling (through specialist shops, pet shops, garden centres, etc), fish husbandry (breeding and looking after stock), and fitting and maintaining special equipment. There are relevant courses at Sparsholt College, Hampshire: contact the college for full information.

GAMEKEEPER

> The gamekeeper's job was originally to provide game for the estate owner and friends to shoot. Now, shooting is big business, and many people will pay large sums of money to spend a day shooting pheasant or grouse, and a day's deer-hunting could cost over a thousand pounds. The gamekeeper is therefore really in the business of livestock production. You may need some good GCSEs or equivalent to get on to an appropriate college course.

The gamekeeper's year is from February to the end of January, when the shooting season ends. The main species which concern the gamekeeper are the pheasant in the lowlands and the grouse on the moors.

What the work involves

The birds have to be reared, often in a hatchery; buildings and equipment must be maintained; predators have to be managed. Throughout the year, the habitats of the birds have to be preserved – overgrown woodland areas must be cleared, and ponds and hedgerows must be maintained.

When the shooting season starts, the keeper has to organise the sport, direct the clients to the right place and organise the beaters. He or she also has to protect the game from poachers – who might well be armed and dangerous. A keeper also needs to be an expert naturalist and competent 'handyperson' and to know about game laws.

Gamekeeping is not a very well-paid job: agricultural wages are usually paid. However, accommodation is usually provided, and sometimes a vehicle, and often cheap or free firewood. Hours are long and often involve working at weekends and bank holidays. For much of the year the life can be lonely. On the other hand, bosses and supervisors won't be breathing down your neck!

GETTING STARTED

Gamekeeping is not an occupation in which opportunities are expanding – rather the reverse. Less than 100 new entrants are needed each year, according to the Game Conservancy.

The traditional way to get started has been to work as an assistant to an experienced keeper, but finding such an apprenticeship can be very difficult. Your local careers service may know of any training placements for young people available in your area.

You can also try approaching gamekeepers and the estate offices of larger estates in your area to see if there is any chance of getting work as an assistant. Weekend beating or helping with pheasant-rearing might be a way of getting yourself known. You will certainly be expected to already have some relevant experience.

COURSES

There are some relevant college courses around. For instance, Askham Bryan College, Newton Rigg College and Sparsholt College offer a range of courses which cover gamekeeping, lasting from one to three years. Entry requirements range from no academic qualifications to a number of good GCSEs or equivalent, including maths and science. Applicants are expected to have had some experience before they start (see the advice in the paragraph above). There are a handful of other courses – including BTEC and City & Guilds qualifications – at colleges in rural areas. Higher National Diploma courses usually require at least one A level or equivalent. See the *Directory of Further Education* at your local library, or the ECCTIS computer database if it is available.

Many of the students will have already had some training, or are mature students. Other agricultural colleges may offer gamekeeping as an option in agricultural courses.

NVQ qualifications are being developed and level 2 (Underkeeper level) and level 3 (Single-handed keeper) are available at some colleges.

The Game Conservancy in Fordingbridge offers short courses for gamekeepers on specialised aspects of the work. These are quite expensive and you would probably have to finance yourself.

WORKING WITH LIVESTOCK IN AGRICULTURE

Agriculture is now a highly mechanised and technological industry. Whatever job you do in farming, it will involve an aspect of this technical revolution, so today's people in farming must be well-trained, well-qualified and adaptable. You can start on the qualifications ladder with just a few GCSEs or equivalent, but the more exam passes you have the better.

Agriculture offers jobs for general farm-hands, skilled workers to look after animals such as pigs and cattle, and unit managers to run sizeable production units. There are also jobs for agricultural advisers and vets, artificial inseminators, milk recorders, market employees, etc, which all involve contact with livestock.

Following the scientific and technological changes of recent decades, the actual number of people engaged in farming work has generally decreased and is continuing to do so. Fewer and fewer people work on the land and only 25% of all UK farms employ regular workers.

What it takes

Agriculture might be the right career for you, if you:

- like the outdoor life – in all weathers!
- can live without the bright lights and amenities of the city;
- are fit and quite strong;
- are a practical person;

- are careful and responsible;
- care about the welfare of animals;
- don't mind working irregular – and often long – hours;
- can work on your own.

Jobs in farming

There are a few jobs in farming for unskilled labourers, with no qualifications at all. But most farm workers come under the following categories:

Craft level

Most practical jobs in farming are carried out by craftsmen and women. Care of livestock (cattle, pigs, sheep, battery hens, etc) and tractor-driving are examples of craft jobs. Craftsmen and women are usually trained to at least the equivalent of a National Vocational Qualification at level 2.

What it takes

- Farming is an outdoor life where you can often find yourself working alone without supervision. As you will be in charge of valuable machinery and animals, you must be a responsible person.
- Besides being practical, unsentimental about animals and with plenty of basic common sense, you need to acquire a lot of knowledge and skills so that you are able to turn your hand to all sorts of jobs when needed and know what to do in unexpected situations. You may have to decide, for instance, whether to call in the vet to an animal which seems sick. Not acting promptly could be very expensive for your boss, but calling the vet unnecessarily will mean an unwanted bill!
- Some jobs are physically demanding – like lifting bags of feed, or helping with calving.
- You should also think how you would cope with working outdoors in all weathers and, often, working irregular hours. There may well be early mornings, late evenings, weekend

work and overtime, as well as special seasonal demands, according to the type of farm.

Safety is very important in farm work. Serious accidents easily happen where workers are careless and don't pay sufficient attention to safety precautions.

Technician/foreman or woman/unit manager

Jobs at this level require a more detailed technical background, plus the ability to supervise the work of other people. To work at this level you will probably need one or more of the following qualifications: a BTEC National Diploma/Certificate, Advanced GNVQ, NVQ level 3, City & Guilds technician qualification, National Certificate in Agriculture plus National Certificate in Farm Management, or an Advanced National Certificate in Agriculture.

The work typically includes:

- planning work schedules;
- looking after and maintaining equipment;
- running a large animal unit;
- some paperwork and often the use of a computer system.

Farm manager

If you want to run a farm, but don't have one in the family, then farm management may be the job for you. There are about 8000 salaried farm managers in the country. But it's competitive getting a job – there may be 100 applicants against you. Farm managers must run a farm profitably, organise the farm workers and deal with financial and business matters, so they have considerable responsibility. Although some farm managers work up from craft level, increasingly they have experience as a unit manager and at least a BTEC National Diploma, Advanced GNVQ, NVQ levels 3 or 4, a BTEC HND or a degree. They may well have a business qualification as well as an agricultural training.

Organic farming

Organic farming, although representing a small proportion of the industry, has become a little more widespread due to a growing public demand for organic produce. Only when the demand rises to a level which can make it a fair economic prospect will the practice become more commonplace.

Training opportunities have improved in recent years. Courses at various institutions include an organic farming option. Detailed information is available from Careers in Landbased Industries. You could also contact WWOOF – Willing Workers On Organic Farms, or the Soil Association (see Further Information section).

Graduate careers

A few graduates with degrees in agriculture go into farm management, but most go into the agricultural service industries, research work, or the farm advisory service. There are also opportunities abroad.

GETTING STARTED

Starting work straight after school

If you don't want to stay in full-time education, the usual way to get started is through work-based training. Trainees gain a wide range of skills in agriculture, agricultural engineering and farm maintenance over a two-year period. This provides a sound basis for craft-level work in farming, with the opportunity to work towards NVQs. Work-based training can provide the practical experience needed to go on to take a National Certificate course.

Modern Apprenticeships in agriculture are now available, with apprentices working towards NVQs at level 3. Applicants need at least three GCSEs at grade D or above in English, maths and a science, or their equivalent, and some relevant experience. The normal starting age is 16 or 17, but older people may be eligible. Your local TEC and careers service will have more information on the availability of Modern Apprenticeships in your area.

Adult entrants

It is not easy for adults to be accepted as trainees in farming, though there are no official age limits. Gaining experience through casual seasonal work might give you a foot in the door. Some adults dream of owning their own farm. There is no easy solution to this. Very few would have sufficient capital to buy a farm and, without experience, this would be an extremely risky venture. Tenancies are also very difficult to get.

The most likely – though certainly not easy – way to gain experience would be to run a smallholding as a spare-time activity, with your income supplemented by another job (your own job or that of a spouse/partner).

Opportunities for adults are likely to be better in the farming services and supply industry, where other experience – e.g. in mechanics, selling or business – can be put to use. Contracting is another possibility.

Training and/or financial help to start up your own business may be available to adults through special government schemes. Get further information from your nearest Jobcentre/Employment Service Office.

NATIONAL VOCATIONAL QUALIFICATIONS

NVQs are designed to show that people have gained particular skills needed in a job. In agriculture, qualifications are available up to NVQ level 3 in crop and livestock production, livestock production, and mechanical field crop production.

There are level 4 qualifications in crop management and livestock management.

FULL-TIME COURSES

Courses at various levels can be followed at agricultural colleges or universities. For full-time courses, it is advisable to gain practical experience in farming before going to college.

BTEC First Diploma in Agriculture
This is a one-year full-time course of use to those who wish to proceed to the National Diploma course but do not have the necessary academic qualifications to do so. The course is being offered by an increasing number of colleges. Completion of the course satisfies most colleges' requirements for prior industrial experience.

National Certificate in Agriculture
This offers one-year full-time practical courses on specific farming topics. No academic qualifications are necessarily required, but colleges may ask for at least GCSE grade E in English, maths and science, or you may have to pass an individual college's entrance test. Here, pre-college industrial experience of one or preferably two years is essential and can most probably be gained through work-based training.

City & Guilds
Full-time and part-time courses in agriculture are offered at various NVQ levels. GCSEs grade D/E or equivalent may be required.

BTEC National and Higher National Diplomas
Courses for potential farm managers, unit managers and other specialists are offered in general agriculture and various specialisms, such as dairying and agricultural merchanting. The entry requirements are four GCSEs at grade C or above for a National Diploma course, plus one A level for an HND

(equivalent GNVQs are also accepted). Subjects offered should include two sciences and a subject which shows command of English. The National Diploma also acts as an entry qualification to the HND.

Degrees
Three-year and four-year sandwich degree courses are offered in both agriculture and agricultural sciences with a minimum educational requirement of five GCSEs at grade C and two A levels or equivalent. Science subjects are important and three A levels are preferable to the minimum of two.

Entry to degree courses can require a pre-course period of full-time experience in the industry, but many courses incorporate practical modules.

Small-scale enterprises

If you only have access to a smallholding, you have to find a niche where you are not competing with large-scale farmers. When experienced farmers are going bankrupt, small-scale concerns certainly have to be well run in order to survive! You may not need qualifications to set up your own rural enterprise, but you will need to know the work you are tackling – and to have done research into running a business.

Free-range eggs will always find a market, as will naturally produced meat. A practical and unsentimental approach is essential. What are you going to do with unwanted cockerels, non-laying hens or billygoat kids? **Rare-breed farms** are popular at the moment and this interest can combine well with breeding animals for food.

Beekeeping is an enjoyable hobby, but is more problematic as a business. Average yields per hive are around 15kg, so hundreds of hives are needed for a respectable income. Unfortunately, average yields conceal the fact that, in some years, not only do you get no honey, but you have to feed the bees as well. Most beekeeping enterprises also sell equipment and bees to amateur beekeepers.

As well as keeping animals for food, there are opportunities on the pet and leisure side. Animal breeding, pet kennels, riding and livery stables are all possibilities on a modest holding.

Agricultural testing and inspecting

Much of the work carried out in agricultural testing and inspecting is concerned with the quality of produce intended for human consumption. Another important test area is the quality and reliability of materials that the farmer uses. Many of the jobs in this area are scientific and technical, based in laboratories, and technician or graduate level qualifications are usually required.

The State Veterinary Service

Qualified vets are employed by the Ministry of Agriculture, Fisheries and Food to deal with such matters as notifiable diseases and animal welfare. They operate controls on the import and export of livestock, and conditions at markets. Ministry vets involved in fieldwork spend much of their time visiting farms. (See earlier section.)

Feedstuffs

A lot of time and effort goes into the formulation of animal feeds. Manufacturing firms need feed analysts and nutrition advisers to carry out experiments to test the quality of their products. Feed manufacturers may have their own experimental farms, as well as contracting out test work to farmers. Testing staff are graduates with suitable degrees in subjects such as animal nutrition, chemistry and biology. There are also opportunities for technician-level staff with about four GCSEs at grade C or above, including science, or an equivalent qualification.

Environmental health

Environmental health officers have responsibilities for farms in the same way as they do for factories. Potentially environmentally-damaging situations must be investigated and sorted out. The Meat Hygiene Service, an agency of MAFF, is responsible for checking conditions in abattoirs.

ZOOS & SAFARI PARKS

In Britain, there are about 150 zoos, safari parks, bird gardens, dolphinariums and aquariums open to the public. About 15 are large zoos and another 20 are specialist bird collections. Only about 2,500 people work in zoos and wildlife collections, and there is much competition for jobs. Keepers don't need any particular qualifications to get started, but there are other jobs for graduates in subjects like zoology or veterinary science to work in research, welfare or education.

Zoo-keeper

The daily work of a zoo-keeper consists of feeding the animals, cleaning out their living quarters, and generally caring for them. It's mucky and strenuous work very often, and it's important to be sensitive to animals – to note changes in their mood or eating habits, and to spot any signs of possible ill health. Keepers learn this only through experience and from knowledge of the individual animals and species in their care. They are involved in the design and landscaping of the animals' environment, based on this knowledge.

Other duties involve looking after sick and injured animals and caring for pregnant females and newly-born young. Sometimes a mother will reject its young and the keeper takes over the job of rearing the young animal by hand.

Keepers normally come into contact with the public as they do their routine work, and are often asked questions about the animals. It's important to be patient and have a pleasant manner with people – especially children – as this affects the zoo's public image. This is especially important in a pet's corner or children's zoo, where domestic animals, birds and other tame species are kept. Keepers supervise donkey and pony rides, and sometimes make an entertainment out of feeding time by holding a chimps' tea party.

Safari park keeper

In safari parks, such as Longleat, most of the animals roam about as if in their natural surroundings. This makes the keeper's job rather different from that in a 'closed' zoo. There is still some cleaning out of cages, etc, as young or sick animals and new arrivals to the park are kept caged. Feeding the animals is dealt with rather differently – at Longleat, keepers tour the park in trucks, hurling out meat that they have prepared to the lions and other animals. A big feature of the keepers' work is looking after the safety of the public, patrolling in jeeps – ready to deal with the rare accident which can happen – and ensuring that the public obey safety rules. Safari park keepers tend to be experienced in other types of zoo work.

In any sort of zoo, the work has to go on seven days a week, including bank holidays and Christmas day! The animals need feeding every day, not just Monday to Friday. As with any other job in the leisure and pleasure industry, the keeper works when other people are on holiday. That's when the zoo makes most of its money. Keepers don't work a seven-day week, of course – there is a rota system for weekends, evenings, bank holidays, etc.

QUALIFICATIONS AND TRAINING

You don't need any particular qualifications to be a zoo-keeper, although most employers prefer several good GCSEs or equivalent. Relevant A levels and/or a degree would be an advantage. Almost all zoos have waiting lists of people wanting to work for them, so get your name on those waiting lists as soon as possible. Some zoos take people from 16 upwards to

train as keepers or animal helpers; others prefer slightly older recruits. Zoos also take temporary staff in the summer to help with cleaning, opening gates, selling tickets, etc, which could provide a toe in the door.

The City & Guilds' Certificate in Animal Management, gained by completing a correspondence course run by the National Extension College, has become widely accepted as an industry standard qualification. National Vocational Qualifications in animal care are available at levels 1 and 2; level 3 equates to the City & Guilds' qualification in animal management. These animal-care NVQs are more general than the NEC course, but are relevant to zoo-keepers.

Trainee keepers are often required to follow and successfully complete a course, and certification is increasingly necessary for transfer to more senior positions. Promotion prospects to senior keeper and head keeper are limited.

You'll need a clean driving licence to work as a safari park keeper.

Other jobs

Large zoos employ small numbers of staff besides keepers:

Laboratory technicians – assist in routine testing and analysis where experimental work or health care is being carried out. At least four GCSEs at grade C or equivalent are required, to include science, English and mathematics. Two science A levels or an Advanced GNVQ in science would be even better. For senior posts, Higher National or professional qualifications may be required.

Animal technicians/veterinary nurses – look after sick animals and those in quarantine and experimental programmes. Four GCSEs at grade C or equivalent are generally required. Zoo nurses are usually keepers as well.

Education officers – prepare educational materials and talk to groups of young people visiting zoos. They are suitably qualified teachers or graduates in a relevant subject.

Zoologists, veterinary surgeons and other qualified graduate scientists – are employed as curators and on research projects, etc, mainly at the larger zoos.

Librarians, administrators and clerical staff – would require the normal qualifications and skills, possibly with some specialist knowledge.

just THE JOB

ZOOLOGY

> A zoologist is a biologist who specialises in the study of animals. This usually means taking a degree course in either biology or zoology. However, a few people who are able to interest the media have become well-known for studies of animal behaviour without having this academic background. You need patience to make accurate observations and recordings, which a good degree course will help you to develop.

Originally, zoologists were natural historians, concerned with finding, naming and classifying the animal world, and a lot of their work involved the dissection of dead animals. Although the identification side is still important, zoology is now more about the critical and caring observation of live animals. The term *animals* does not just mean furry mammals. Parasitic mites, limpets and even single-celled creatures such as the amoeba come into the province of the zoologist.

What do zoologists do?
- They try to understand animal behaviour.
- They develop simple systems through which to communicate with animals.
- They investigate how the structure of parts of animals are related to their functioning.
- They observe the interaction of animals with each other, with other species and with their environment.

TAKING A ZOOLOGY COURSE

Some of the topics studied on a zoology course include:

- animal classification (vertebrate and invertebrate groups);
- cell biology;
- vertebrate and invertebrate structure and function: studying the anatomy and workings of their respiratory, circulatory, feeding, excretory and reproduction systems;
- animal control systems (control of their internal environment through the nervous and endocrine or hormonal systems);
- animal behaviour and locomotion;
- developmental and reproductive biology;
- genetics;
- evolutionary theory and palaeozoology (the study of fossil animals);
- ecology;
- laboratory practice;
- data collection and data-handling techniques.

The course may involve particular studies, such as entomology (insects) and ornithology (study of birds and their behaviour).

Zoology is a wide subject, taught through lectures, seminars and a great deal of practical work conducted both in the field and in the laboratory. Individual and team projects form an essential part of the course-work, with field studies often running through vacations.

COURSES

Many universities and colleges offer courses in zoology, sometimes combined with other subjects. In general, you will need a minimum of five GCSEs at grade C, plus at least two A levels (often three). The best combination of subjects would include A level chemistry and biology and GCSE level mathematics.

You could offer zoology A level instead of biology. While A level chemistry allows the best selection of courses, it is not absolutely essential, but GCSE at grade C or double science with a high chemistry content is. A knowledge of physics is also of great assistance in physiological work. For information on courses see the CRAC *Degree Course Guide: Biology*, available in most careers and public libraries.

Martin – zoologist

'My decision at eighteen to take a zoology degree has led me to the point where I know every black rhinoceros in Namibia (there are about two hundred, by the way). After I had completed my first degree I realised that, if I was to have a career in zoology I would need to get a higher degree. I decided to do some research to get myself a PhD. I also decided I would like to travel as well, so I picked on a rather unlikely and mysterious animal called the giant mole rat. This was attractive, not for its appearance which is best described as a giant white slug with teeth, but because it was little understood or studied, and could be found in Kenya.

I did find out some very interesting things about this curious animal, which lives in colonies with a queen rather like bees, and I did get my PhD. Perhaps more important was the contacts I made in Kenya which led to my first job. The Kenyan wildlife authorities were very worried about their declining rhino population, which were being poached for their horns. They needed to know how many they had, where they were and information such as the age and sex structure of the population. They needed zoologists and so, being on the spot, I became a junior assistant on the project. I had to develop many new skills, such as firing anaesthetic darts at rhinos, taking *blood samples once they had keeled over and judging when to get away before they came round and got annoyed. Kenyan rhinos, because of the amount of hunting they endured, were very bad tempered. Our team, having researched the problems, also had to come up with possible solutions, and I was then involved in setting up protected reserves for the remaining animals.*

Once this contract was completed (and it was a four-year job), I had to look round for something else. Fortunately the world of rhino experts is relatively small, so when the fairly newly independent country of Namibia decided it too needed to find out something about its population of the increasingly threatened black rhino, I was a strong candidate. Now, however, instead of being the junior assistant, I am in charge and responsible for deciding how to run the project and spend the money in the best way. More new skills are needed, including, because of the large size of the country, learning to fly a light plane.

The problem with my job, fascinating and demanding thought it is, is the short-term nature of the contracts; this one finishes in a year's time. I am now married with a family and I may have eventually to look for something more conventional and settled. I hope the rhinos don't miss me too much! '

EMPLOYMENT FOR ZOOLOGISTS

Finding a job which is based primarily on zoology is not easy and you may well need to take a higher degree (an MSc or a PhD) to specialise in a particular area. This means first getting a good BSc degree. You might improve your employment prospects by taking an applied zoology course (e.g. agricultural zoology, animal physiology). Many zoology graduates go into occupations that are not directly related to their studies.

Jobs specifically concerned with zoology are often in research in higher education, government service or agricultural research. Research topics include animals of economic importance and pests and diseases. There are always more graduates looking for this sort of job than there are posts available. The same is true of jobs in ecology and conservation. Research jobs are usually offered for the funding period of a research grant, with little opportunity of subsequent full-time work.

All the jobs open to biology/life science graduates are also possibilities for zoology graduates. These include working with the water companies, the Environment Agency, medical research (including cancer research, immunology and parasitology), commercial fish-farming, or working in manufacturing industries testing and developing products.

MARINE & FRESHWATER BIOLOGY

> Marine and freshwater biology is the study of plant and animal life in the sea, rivers and lakes. The range of living things in a water system gives vital information about its level of purity or pollution. Most jobs in this field are for graduates in biological sciences, but there are also openings for technicians and laboratory assistants with lower qualifications.

The majority of human activities have an eventual effect upon the delicate balance of the earth's water cycles. Any alteration to levels of dissolved chemicals, or to the acidity or alkalinity of a water system, affects the survival of living things – being themselves nearly 90% water.

Some problem areas for biologists

- Industrial activity, domestic heating systems and combustion engines pump out acid gases which dissolve in rain water and cause direct or indirect damage to wildlife.
- Nuclear power stations are responsible for seepage of radio-activity into marine waters, causing harm to the natural environment.
- Oil refineries, power stations and industrial plants often release very hot water, and other effluents, into rivers and estuaries, which has a damaging effect on the life in those waters.
- The use of pesticides and artificial fertilisers is having serious consequences on food chains which start in freshwater

systems. These chemicals may cause fertility problems and, possibly, cancers in man.
- Roadside run-off and the waters collecting in storm gullies are contaminated by poisonous heavy metal particles from vehicle emissions and tyres.
- Water companies are having to tap the underlying water tables to keep up with customer demand. Some surface rivers have permanently disappeared.
- Heavy fishing has reduced worldwide stocks of particular fish species.

Concern over these matters, or an interest in leisure activities associated with waterways, has made this area of applied biology a popular career choice. The opportunity of doing a job with a lot of outdoor work, perhaps including fishing and messing about in boats, is possibly a reason why students are attracted to the subject. But don't be misled into thinking it's a soft option. Sampling estuarine mud to work out the distribution of lugworms throughout a period of twenty-four hours is not always comfortable or agreeable!

Who employs marine and freshwater biologists?

Most employment for marine and freshwater biologists is in research and development. This could be what is called *pure research*, examining basic problems of the science, or *applied research*, using the results of pure research to solve practical problems and to develop and improve industries based on marine and freshwater life.

There are a number of organisations involved in applied research. Some, like the Natural Environment Research Council, have a wide range of interests; others are more specifically concerned with one area. The Ministry of Agriculture, Fisheries and Food, for example, is concerned with *edible* marine life. Freshwater biologists are also employed by water companies and the Environment Agency. Commercial fisheries and large industrial concerns are other possible employers.

QUALIFICATIONS AND COURSES

There may be a few openings at the scientific technician and laboratory assistant level for those with four science GCSEs at grade C, which include double science and mathematics. Students who have an A level in biology (or an equivalent qualification, such as a BTEC National Diploma/Certificate or an Advanced GNVQ) might also work as technicians, but the current trend is to employ those trained to a higher level of specialism in biology.

A BTEC Higher National Diploma in applied biology is a useful qualification. HND courses require four GCSEs at grade C and A level biology (and chemistry studied to A level). There is not much chance of getting a place on a biology course unless you can demonstrate a reasonable competence in chemistry.

The usual requirement for professional workers in this field is a degree in biology or biochemistry. A special interest in marine or freshwater studies would of course be helpful. For most biology degrees, a minimum of two A levels and five GCSEs at grade C is required. A levels should preferably include biology and chemistry, although some courses will accept chemistry at GCSE only.

There are a few courses leading to first degrees in marine or freshwater biology. It is also worth checking prospectuses for details of biology courses which offer marine/freshwater studies, ecology or environmental studies as options. For information on courses and requirements, consult up-to-date editions of *University and College Entrance* and *Compendium of Higher Education*. You can also use the ECCTIS computer database, if

available, to find out about courses. The CRAC *Degree Course Guide: Biology* will help you find suitable courses.

A biology first degree can be followed by a higher degree specialising in marine/freshwater biology, and several universities and colleges offer such courses.

JOB PROSPECTS

There are more qualified people trying to work in marine and freshwater biology than can be absorbed. This is a particular problem at the moment, as many of the employing organisations are government-run or government-funded and their recruiting programmes have suffered cutbacks. It is advisable to start with a broad-based qualification, rather than specialising too early and so limiting your future employment prospects.

NATURE CONSERVATION

Many jobs in nature conservation are only indirectly concerned with animals, as the focus is on conserving the *environment* for wildlife, rather than the wildlife itself. There are several organisations whose work is to protect and care for the countryside in which we live. These statutory bodies employ scientific officers who have responsibility for the management of nature reserves. Rangers, administrative staff and practical workers look after the areas on a day-to-day basis, and may have qualifications ranging from none at all to postgraduate level.

The Countryside Commission

The Countryside Commission is concerned with conserving and enhancing the beauty of the English countryside and improving countryside leisure facilities. The Commission owns no land, but designates grant aid for projects and gives advice on defining Heritage coastlines, establishing national trails, running the national parks, and maintaining long-distance footpaths, bridle-paths and areas of outstanding natural beauty. Funding comes directly from the Department of the Environment.

Only about 330 staff work for the Commission. Some of this number work at the headquarters in Cheltenham, while over half are occupied in the seven regional offices which put Commission policy into practice. The specialists are planners, landscape architects, economists and graduates in life/biological sciences (e.g. botany, environmental sciences). There are also staff concerned with publicity, and others who provide information and training for people working in conservation.

English Nature

English Nature is responsible for developing and running over 170 national nature reserves, and advising the government on conservation issues. It employs scientific staff who are mainly graduates, and who are usually given responsibility for planning and management of nature conservation sites, on a county basis. This entails a lot of liaison work – with local authority planning departments, landowners of designated sites, voluntary conservation bodies, and so on. They also do assessments and surveys of Sites of Special Scientific Interest (SSSIs), and develop conservation education. Applicants should normally be under 30 with a degree in life/environmental science. An MSc in conservation or ecology could well be advantageous, but any postgraduate experience gained voluntarily would help.

English Nature's national nature reserves are managed by **site managers** (formerly called reserve wardens). Their work includes management planning, scientific monitoring of species and habitats, and liaison work with landowners, tenants and occupiers, and other conservation bodies. They show visiting groups around reserves, and prepare and maintain facilities, like nature trails, for the general public. Site managers are also responsible for the supervision of estate workers, voluntary wardens, volunteer groups and contractors. It is a mixture of office-based and outdoor work, including weekends and evenings.

Site managers are usually appointed in their twenties or thirties. They need a driving licence and a keen, all-round interest in nature conservation. Experience is valuable – as a voluntary ranger/in estate work/in forestry – and, although no academic qualifications are essential, qualifications of A-level standard, or a degree in an appropriate subject, are highly advantageous.

Estate workers who do manual jobs such as hedging and ditching, clearing and tree-felling are also needed occasionally. There are administrative and clerical staff, who include land agents, accountants and general administrators.

The Forestry Commission

The Forestry Commission is made up of two parts:

Forest Authority

This is the *advisory* part of the Forestry Commission and owns no land. It offers advice to landowners in the private sector. It gives grants for planting and carries out research into many related areas such as woodland, its wildlife and the use of chemicals. The Authority employs foresters, research scientists and practical workers.

Forest Enterprise

This is the *management* side of the Forestry Commission. Forest Enterprise owns and manages many forests. Job openings are for administrators, scientists on research stations, forest officers for management and planning, and foresters with a National Diploma or degree in forestry, or possibly a Full Forestry Certificate. Forestry foremen and women with at least NVQ level 2 in forestry are in charge of the day-to-day work, including ground-level wildlife conservation. It also employs landscape architects, land agents and rangers.

There are three different types of ranger. **Wildlife rangers** are involved in the control of wild animals like deer and squirrels, and in conservation projects. No formal qualifications are required. **Recreation managers** are involved in recreation facilities, and the education of the general public and visiting schoolchildren. These posts usually require a qualification such as a BTEC National Diploma in Countryside Recreation. **Conservation rangers** are involved in specific conservation schemes, surveys, etc. They generally have degrees or HNDs.

Forest workers include skilled and unskilled practical workers who carry out tree planting and felling, clearing, weeding of saplings, etc. Most of this work is done by outside contractors.

The National Parks
There are managerial and administrative posts similar to those in the other organisations. The work involves liaison with the owners of land falling within the National Park boundaries, buying and developing land, and the overall management of the parks. There are occasional vacancies for fully trained planners, leisure and recreation managers, surveyors, estate managers, conservation specialists, etc. Information and publicity are also very important to the National Parks' work – providing facilities for huge numbers of visitors, displays, information guides, running gift shops, educational facilities and so on. Some jobs are seasonal and temporary – e.g. helping with an information centre in the busy summer months. Wardens and rangers guide visitors, look after wildlife and carry out conservation policy on a day-to-day basis. Weekend, seasonal staff and volunteers are used too, and this type of work can give valuable experience.

The National Trust
The National Trust is a large landowner as well as the guardian of many historic houses. The Trust's land is precious both as landscape and as unspoilt natural habitat. For example, much of the country's unimproved lowland meadows are Trust property. Agents and wardens of the Trust are therefore deeply involved in conservation work. Opportunities with the Trust are limited and there is a lot of competition for jobs. Senior posts need excellent qualifications in science, agriculture or estate management, combined with practical experience. The Trust also employs archaeologists, gardeners, forestry staff, building maintenance staff, public relations officers, and financial, administrative and retailing staff.

There are a limited number of training opportunities for school-leavers wanting a career in amenity gardening or as a countryside warden in a scheme called *Careership*. The scheme runs for three years, working towards NVQ level 3. Academic requirements are four GCSEs at grade C, including maths or science, plus English.

Environment Agency

This is the body which regulates the environment, by protecting and enhancing the land, water and air. The Agency's functions include conservation, fisheries, waste regulation, flood defence, recreation, navigation and pollution prevention and control. As well as the Bristol headquarters, there are other regional centres. Most jobs are for scientists to carry out the monitoring. They also employ **water bailiffs** whose work involves keeping rivers well stocked and enforcing fishing legislation.

Other opportunities to do with nature conservation

There are many opportunities for voluntary work and, very occasionally, paid posts arise with voluntary bodies and pressure groups.

The Wildlife Trusts are a nationwide network of local trusts which work to protect wildlife in town and country. The trusts employ approximately 600 people, but many posts are temporary. Joining your local trust will give you an insight into the work involved, and voluntary work experience is valuable when applying for paid employment.

Local authorities in rural areas employ wardens and rangers to oversee rights of way and open spaces.

The Farming and Wildlife Advisory Group employs a small number of farm conservation advisers to encourage nature conservation on farms. Applicants need to be over 25 and have relevant qualifications and experience.

The Natural Environment Research Council (NERC) is the UK's leading body for environmental research, surveys and monitoring. The Council has a role in training in the environmental sciences, and employs scientists in a wide range of disciplines, as well as technical, administrative and support staff. Jobs also sometimes arise in industry – with firms who feel a responsibility to research the effect of their operations on wildlife; and in education – in schools and colleges, through lectures and activities with children and adults in their leisure time, etc. Some qualified teachers work as education officers for conservation bodies.

There are a few opportunities for training in nature conservation with an employer – ask at your local careers office for details – and some opportunities (mainly practical) for adults on the government's training schemes. Make enquiries at your local Jobcentre/Employment Services Office.

COURSES

There is a wide range of appropriate BTEC courses, first degree-level and postgraduate courses in biological and environmental sciences, forestry, estate management, etc. GNVQs in Land and Environment are being introduced in some schools and colleges. For a comprehensive list of courses, consult the Environmental Council's *Directory of Environmental Courses* (see Further Information section).

ANIMAL TECHNICIAN

> Some people will be surprised to find this sort of work included in a book about working with animals, as they may feel very strongly about animals being used for these purposes. Staff involved in experimental work certainly need an unsentimental attitude to the animals they use in laboratories, but many staff still feel a strong concern for the welfare of the animals, within the limits of the work which they do. Most technicians have at least some good GCSEs, followed by further qualifications gained on-the-job.

In Britain, over three million laboratory animals are used each year in medical and veterinary investigation and research. The animals used are raised and cared for by animal technicians, who may also assist with experiments. Many different types of animals are used for research purposes: mainly mice and rats, but also rabbits, hamsters, guinea pigs, monkeys, dogs, cats and farmyard animals.

The number of experimental procedures on animals has decreased in recent years as alternative methods are found, but animal experiments are unlikely to be replaced entirely in the foreseeable future. There are strict controls and regulations concerning the use of animals in laboratories.

Animal technician work includes breeding, looking after newborn animals, feeding, cleaning out cages, attending to sick animals and keeping records of animal behaviour and health.

Technicians can work in hospitals, universities, pharmaceutical companies, private research organisations and with some government-financed establishments involved in medical research and public health services. Experienced technicians can be promoted to senior and chief animal technician and departmental supervisors.

What it takes

It is important to be interested in and to respect animals. Their day-to-day welfare is the technician's responsibility. But remember that the animals with which technicians work are used in experimental procedures. If you have a sentimental affection for animals, or are unhappy about animal experiments, you would be unlikely to want to do this work, though practising technicians like to be satisfied that the scientific procedures in which they are involved are really necessary. You should be prepared to do some dirty and menial work, and to work at weekends when needed.

EDUCATION AND TRAINING

It is not essential to have any educational qualifications to get a job as an animal technician, though many employers will ask for GCSEs at grade C and perhaps A levels/BTEC National, or Advanced GNVQ in science. GCSEs in English, mathematics and science subjects are certainly an advantage in getting a job.

Training is usually by means of a combination of on-the-job instruction and part-time education. Part-time courses, which are held at a few colleges nationally, lead to the Institute of Animal Technology's qualifications. It is also possible to study for these qualifications through open or distance learning. An alternative qualification offered by some colleges is the BTEC National Certificate in Science (Animal Technology), which can also be a route to membership of the Institute.

Qualified veterinary nurses and holders of some animal husbandry diplomas may be allowed exemption from parts of the course.

There are also BTEC Higher National Certificates which are recognised by the Institute. Further courses offered by the Institute lead to Fellowship examinations.

OTHER OPPORTUNITIES FOR WORKING WITH ANIMALS

Pet shops
Pet shops are mostly very small family businesses, but they sometimes advertise for staff. As for any shop work, you need a reasonable standard in English and maths, and an interest in biology is useful. A Saturday job or holiday job could be a good way in – ask around.

A typical pet shop sells all kinds of small animals, fish and birds, as well as pet accessories such as food, cages, baskets, etc. As well as serving in the shop, pet shop assistants usually care for the animals – feeding them, cleaning them out, watching for signs of disease, and so on. Staff can take a correspondence course which leads to a City & Guilds certificate in pet store management. For more information, write to the Pet Care Trust.

Personal qualities rather than academic qualifications are the priority for this sort of work. Hours of work can vary considerably.

People who work in shops can study on a part-time basis for the examinations of awarding bodies such as City & Guilds, LCCI and Pitmans. There are NVQs at levels 1–4 in Retailing. Ask at your local college of further education for details.

Taxidermist
These are the craftspeople who mount and stuff dead animals to make them look natural. The resulting objects are usually displayed in museums and private collections. Taxidermists can be

self-employed, or employed by museums. Very few people do this work, which requires a keen interest in nature, but it's highly rewarding if you have the right skills (see *Working with your Hands* in the *Just the Job!* series).

Working in the media

There are opportunities for specialising in animals or natural history in career areas like journalism, illustration, broadcasting and photography.

There are two main routes into these areas. Some people who happen to have an interest in animals may follow a normal training course in art, photography, sound recording or whatever; once they have acquired the right technical skills, and experience in using them in other fields, they may be able to exploit opportunities for involvement with animals as they arise. Or you could get there from the opposite direction: if your first expertise lies in your knowledge of animals, then it is the filming, writing techniques, etc, which you pick up as you go along. Thus these media jobs tend to be 'second career' activities, in the sense that you have to start somewhere else first.

For those with suitable knowledge and abilities, there can be all sorts of opportunities – editing, writing and taking photographs for leisure interest publications, illustrating adult and children's books, etc. For information on training in journalism, broadcasting, etc, see *Information & the Written Word* in the *Just the Job!* series.

Note for adult readers
As has been mentioned, although there are a lot of different types of work with animals, overall they do not account for a great many jobs. There is usually quite a lot of competition for those which occur. When it comes to formal training courses, adults may find that their maturity and experience mean that stated entry requirements can be waived for them.

FOR FURTHER INFORMATION

GENERAL
Animal Care Industry Lead Body – College of Animal Welfare, Wood Green Animal Shelter, Godmanchester, Huntingdon PE18 8LJ. Tel: 01480 831177 (For information on NVQs in animal care and relevant courses.)

Careers in Landbased Industries – Warwickshire Careers Service, 10 Northgate Street, Warwick CV34 4SR. Tel: 01926 412427.

Universities' Federation for Animal Welfare (UFAW) – 8 Hamilton Close, South Mimms, Potters Bar, Hertfordshire EN6 3QD. Tel: 01707 658202. The Federation researches, reports, and give guidance on the welfare of animals as pets, and in zoos, farms and laboratories. Send 50p in stamps for a leaflet on careers with animals.

Zoological Society of London – London Zoo, Regent's Park, London NW1 4RY. Tel: 0171 722 3333. Enclose a stamped, addressed envelope with queries.

Careers Working with Animals, published by Kogan Page.
Careers with Animals, available from the Universities' Federation for Animal Welfare (address above).
Working in Work with Animals, published by COIC.

VETERINARY WORK
British Veterinary Nursing Association – D12, The Seedbed Centre, Coldharbour Road, Harlow, Essex CM19 5AF. Tel: 01279 450567. The BVNA runs an employment register and provides a (priced) list of approved training centres. For careers literature and information about the VN training scheme, send a large, stamped self-addressed envelope.

Royal College of Veterinary Surgeons – Education Department, Belgravia House, 62–64 Horse Ferry Road, London SW1P 2AF. Tel: 0171 222 2001. Publishes *A Career as a Veterinary Surgeon*, a detailed guide (priced) to training and career opportunities.

University of Bristol School of Veterinary Science – Veterinary Nursing Unit, Langford House, Langford, nr Bristol, BS18 7DU. Tel: 0117 928 9517.

The CRAC *Degree Course Guide: Veterinary Science* will help you choose your course. This publication is available in most school, college and careers service libraries.

The leaflet *Careers as Veterinary Surgeon, Veterinary Nurse or Animal Technician* is available from Careers in Landbased Industries (address above): send a stamped, addressed envelope.

Veterinary Record, which is published weekly for veterinary surgeons, lists job vacancies.

ANIMAL WELFARE

Blue Cross – Field Centre, Shilton Road, Burford, Oxfordshire OX18 4PF. Tel: 01993 822651. Stamped, addressed envelopes are appreciated.

People's Dispensary for Sick Animals – Whitechapel Way, Priorslee, Telford, Shropshire TF2 9PQ. Tel: 01952 290999.

Royal Society for the Prevention of Cruelty to Animals, - Causeway, Horsham, West Sussex RH12 1HG. Tel: 01403 223284. The RSPCA produces the leaflets *Working for the RSPCA – a career in the inspectorate* and *So you want to work with animals*.

WORKING WITH DOGS AND CATS

Animal Care College – Ascot House, Ascot, Berkshire SL5 7JG. Tel: 01344 28269.

Bell Mead Training College for Kennelstaff – Priest Hill House, Old Windsor, Berkshire SL4 2JN. Tel: 01784 432929.

British Association of Dogs' Homes – Dogs Home Battersea, Battersea Park Road, London SW8 4AA. Tel: 0171 622 3626.

Guide Dogs for the Blind Association – Hillfields, Burghfield, Reading RG7 3YG. Tel: 01734 835555.
Hearing Dogs for the Deaf – Training Centre, London Road (A40), Lewknor, Oxfordshire OX9 5RY. Tel: 01844 353898.
Kennel Club – 1 Clarges Street, Piccadilly, London W1Y 8AB. Tel: 0171 493 6651.
National Canine Defence League – 17 Wakley Street, London EC1V 7LT. Tel: 0171 837 0006.
National Dog Wardens Association – The Secretary, 22 Stubbs Hill, Dorking, Surrey RH4 2QD.
National Greyhound Racing Club Ltd – 24–28 Oval Road, London NW1 7DA. Tel: 0171 267 9256.
Pet Care Trust – Bedford Business Centre, 170 Mile Road, Bedford MK42 9TW. Tel: 01234 273933.

Vacancies are advertised in *Dog World*, *Our Dogs* and *Horse and Hound*.

Cats Protection League – 17 Kings Road, Horsham, West Sussex RH13 5PN. Tel: 01403 221900.
Feline Advisory Bureau & Boarding Cattery Information Service – 1 Church Close, Orcheston, Nr Salisbury, Wiltshire. SP3 4RP. Tel: 01980 621201 (Enclose a stamped, addressed envelope).

Running your own Boarding Kennels, published by Kogan Page.

WORKING WITH HORSES

Association of British Riding Schools – Queens Chamber, 38–40 Queen Street, Penzance, Cornwall TR18 4BH. Tel: 01736 69440.
British Horse Society – British Equestrian Centre, Stoneleigh, Kenilworth, Warwickshire CV8 2LR. Tel: 01203 696697.
British Racing School – Snailwell Road, Newmarket CB8 7NU. Tel: 01638 665103.
Farriery Training Service – Sefton House, Adam Court, Newark Road, Peterborough PE1 5PP. Tel: 01733 319770.

Fortune Centre of Riding Therapy – Avon Tyrrell, Bransgore, Christchurch, Dorset BH23 8EE. Tel: 01425 673297.

National Association of Farriers, Blacksmiths and Agricultural Engineers – The Forge, Avenue B, 10th Street, National Agricultural Centre, Stoneleigh, Kenilworth CV8 2LG. Tel: 01203 696595.

National Horse Education and Training Company Ltd – 2nd Floor, Burgess Building, The Green, Stafford ST17 4BL. Tel: 01785 227399.

National Pony Society – Willingdon House, 102 High Street, Alton, Hampshire GU34 1EN. Tel: 01420 88333.

National Stud – Newmarket, Suffolk CB8 0XE. Tel: 01638 663464.

Northern Racing College – The Stables, Rossington Hall, Great North Road, Doncaster, South Yorkshire DN11 0HN. Tel: 01302 865462

Racing and Thoroughbred Breeding Training Board (RTBTB) – Suite 16, Unit 8, Kings Court, Willie Snaith Road, Newmarket, Suffolk CB8 7SG. Tel: 01638 560743.

Riding for the Disabled Association – Avenue R, National Agricultural Centre, Kenilworth, Warwickshire CV8 2LY. Tel: 01203 696510.

Rural Development Commission – 141 Castle Street, Salisbury, Wiltshire SP1 3TP. Tel: 01722 336255.

Vacancies are advertised in *Horse and Hound, Horse and Pony, Riding* and *Sporting Life*.

The British Horse Society publishes various booklets, including, *Careers with Horses* and *Working with Horses*.

CAREERS IN ORNITHOLOGY

British Trust for Ornithology – The Nunnery, Nunnery Place, Thetford, Norfolk IP24 2PU. Tel: 01842 750050.

Royal Society for the Protection of Birds – The Lodge, Sandy, Bedfordshire SG19 2DL. Tel: 01767 680551. (A priced booklet is available on *Careers in Conservation*.)

WATCH – 22 The Green, Witham Park, Lincoln LN5 5RR. Tel: 01522 54400.
Wildfowl and Wetlands Trust – Slimbridge, Gloucester GL2 7BT. Tel: 01453 890333.
Young Ornithologists' Club – contact the RSPB at the above address.

Vacancies are advertised in *Birds*, the *Guardian* and *New Scientist*. Educational posts may be advertised in the *Times Educational Supplement*.

WORK WITH FISH
Environment Agency – Rio House, Waterside Drive, Aztec West, Almondsbury, Bristol BS12 4UD. Tel: 01454 624400.
Institute of Fisheries Management – 22 Rushworth Avenue, West Bridgford, Nottingham NG2 7LF. Tel: 0115 945 5722. Produce a booklet *Careers in Fisheries*.
Ministry of Agriculture, Fisheries and Food (MAFF) – Directorate of Fisheries Research – Pakefield Road, Lowestoft NR33 0HT. Tel: 01502 524334. Is mostly concerned with sea fishing but also conducts research into freshwater fish and their environment.
Sparsholt College – Sparsholt, near Winchester, Hampshire SO21 2NF. Tel: 01962 776441.

GAMEKEEPING
Askham Bryan College – York YO2 3PR. Tel: 01904 702121.
British Association for Shooting & Conservation – Marford Mill, Rossett, Wrexham LL12 0HL. Tel: 01244 573000. Produces a booklet on careers in gamekeeping.
Game Conservancy Trust – Fordingbridge, Hampshire SP6 1EF. Tel: 01425 652381. Enclose a stamped, addressed envelope for general information and course details.
Newton Rigg College – Penrith, Cumbria CA11 0AH. Tel: 01768 63791.
Sparsholt College – Sparsholt, near Winchester, Hampshire SO21 2NF. Tel: 01962 776441.

Vacancies are advertised in the *Shooting Times* (weekly).

WORKING WITH LIVESTOCK IN AGRICULTURE
Careers in Landbased Industries – c/o Warwickshire Careers Service Ltd, 10 Northgate Street, Warwick CV34 4SR. Tel: 01926 412427 to contact Derek Sharman. He prefers to deal with written enquiries enclosing a stamped, addressed envelope.
Food and Farming Information Service – The National Agricultural Centre, Stoneleigh Park, Warwickshire CV8 2LZ. Tel: 01203 535707.
Organic Food and Farming Centre, The Soil Association – 86 Colston Street, Bristol BS1 5BB. Tel: 0117 929 0661.
Willing Workers on Organic Farms (WWOOF) – 19 Bradford Road, Lewes, East Sussex BN7 1RB. Send a stamped, addressed envelope for information. Tel: 01273 476236.

Working in Agriculture and Horticulture, published by COIC.

ZOOS AND SAFARI PARKS
Association of British Wild Animal Keepers – c/o 12 Tackley Road, Eastville, Bristol BS5 6UQ (please send a stamped, addressed envelope). Tel: 0117 951 5950.
Federation of Zoological Gardens of GB & Ireland – Regent's Park, London NW1 4RY. Tel: 0171 586 0230.
Zoological Society of London (Regent's Park/Whipsnade), Regent's Park, London NW1 4RY. Tel: 0171 722 3333.

There are two magazines of relevance to zoo-keepers which carry news, features and some vacancies. The Association of British Wild Animal Keepers publishes *Ratel*; and the Federation of Zoological Gardens of Great Britain and Ireland publishes *Zoo Federation News*.

MARINE AND FRESHWATER BIOLOGY
Institute of Biology – 20 Queensberry Place, London SW7 2DZ. Tel: 0171 581 8333. Produces a set of careers literature, including a (priced) booklet *Careers with Biology*.

Natural Environment Research Council – Polaris House, North Star Avenue, Swindon SN2 1EU. Tel: 01793 411500. Gives information on many freshwater research institutes and marine laboratories which it funds, and information on recruitment.

Nature Conservation

Association of Countryside Rangers – 60 Defoe Drive, Park Hill, West Coyney, Stoke on Trent ST3 5RS. Tel: 01782 316046.

British Trust for Conservation Volunteers – 36 St Mary's St, Wallingford, Oxford OX10 0EU. Tel: 01491 839766. Information on conservation working holidays, volunteer opportunities, and a booklet on practical training courses, *Developing Skills*.

Council for Environmental Education – University of Reading, London Road, Reading, RG1 5AQ. Send a stamped, addressed envelope with enquiry.

Countryside Commission – John Dower House, Crescent Place, Cheltenham, Gloucester GL50 3RA. Tel: 01242 521381. Produces an extensive number of information booklets and guides, including *Employment and Training Opportunities in the Countryside*. For a free copy of the Commission's publication catalogue, write to: Countryside Commission Postal Sales, PO Box 124, Walgrave, Northampton NN6 9TL. Tel: 01604 781848.

Countryside Council for Wales – Plas Penrhos, Fford Penrhos, Bangor, Gwynedd LL57 2LQ. Tel: 01248 385500.

Countryside Management Association – c/o Centre for Environmental Interpretation, Manchester Metropolitan University, St Augustine's, Lower Chatham Street, Manchester M15 6BY. Tel: 0161 247 1067. Send a stamped, addressed A5 envelope, if requesting careers information.

English Nature – Enquiry Service, Northminster House, Peterborough PE1 1UA. Tel: 01733 318252. Contact for a catalogue covering their range of publications.

Environment Agency – Rio House, Waterside Drive, Aztec West, Almondsbury, Bristol BS12 4UD. Tel: 01454 624400.

Environment Council – 21 Elizabeth Street, London SW1W 9RP. Tel: 0171 824 8411. Produces the *Directory of Environmental Courses*, free on receipt of a stamped (83p), addressed A4 envelope. Also publishes *Who's Who in the Environment* (priced).

Environmental Education Council for Wales – 10 Stryd Aberhonddu, Treganna, Cardiff CF5 1RE.

Environmental Training Organisation – The Red House, Pillows Green, Staunton, Gloucester GL19 3NU. Tel: 01452 840825.

Farming and Wildlife Advisory Group – National Agricultural Centre, Stoneleigh, Kenilworth, Warwickshire CV8 2RX. Tel: 01203 696699.

Forestry Commission – 231 Corstophine Road, Edinburgh EH12 7AT. Tel: 0131 334 0303.

Institute of Leisure and Amenity Management – ILAM House, Lower Basildon, Reading, Berkshire RG8 9NE. Tel: 01491 874222. Runs a project-based professional qualifications scheme which can be adapted for those working in the area of conservation.

National Trust – 36 Queen Anne's Gate, Westminster, London SW1H 9AS. Tel: 0171 222 9251. For details of the Careership scheme, contact the National Trust, Careership Office, Lanhydrock, Bodmin, Cornwall PL30 4DE. Tel: 01208 74281.

Natural Environment Research Council – Polaris House, North Star Avenue, Swindon SN2 1EU. Address careers enquiries to Mr M. Nettleford. Tel: 01793 411500.

Scottish Natural Heritage – 12 Hope Terrace, Edinburgh EH9 2AS. Tel: 0131 447 4784. Produces a useful monthly magazine, and *Who's Who in Scotland*, obtainable from the Publications Section, Battleby, Redgorton, Perth PH1 3EW. Tel: 01738 627921.

Wildlife Trusts – The Green, Witham Park, Waterside South, Lincoln LN5 7JR. Tel: 01522 544400. Send a stamped, addressed envelope for information.

WWF UK (World Wide Fund for Nature) – Panda House, Catteshall Lane, Godalming, Surrey GU7 1XR. Tel: 01483 426444.

Environmental Careers Handbook, published by Trotman for the Institution of Environmental Sciences.
Working in the Environment, published by COIC.
Careers in Environmental Conservation, published by Kogan Page.
Careers in Conservation, published by the RSPB, The Lodge, Sandy, Bedfordshire SG19 2DL.

Job vacancies may be advertised in *New Scientist*, *Nature* and the national newspapers, as well as in the Environmental Council's magazine, *Habitat*. The Countryside Management Association (address above) runs a Jobs Advisory Service.

ANIMAL TECHNICIAN
Institute of Animal Technology – 5 South Parade, Summertown, Oxford OX2 7JL.

OTHER WORK WITH ANIMALS
Guild of Taxidermists – Glasgow Art Gallery & Museum, Kelvingrove, Glasgow G3 8AG. Tel: 0141 287 2671.
Pet Care Trust – Bedford Business Centre, 170 Mile Road, Bedford MK42 9TW. Tel: 01234 273933.